# TRANSFER
### *in Kashi*
### *and*
### *the River*
### *of Time*

# TRANSFER
### in *Kashi*
### and the *River*
### of *Time*

## BJORG BJARNADOTTIR

PARTRIDGE

A Penguin Random House Company

ISBN:        Hardcover        978-1-4828-4051-3
             Softcover        978-1-4828-4050-6
             eBook            978-1-4828-4049-0

**To order additional copies of this book, contact**
Partridge India
000 800 10062 62
orders.india@partridgepublishing.com

www.partridgepublishing.com/india

# Contents

For Animal Tamer

# Animal Tamer and a Spirit Grandfather

A boy of eight has the humble dream of becoming an animal tamer. And I fulfill a lifelong dream of visiting the oldest city in the world, Kashi in India aka Banares aka today's Varanasi.

I had felt the need to visit the city of final transfer after the death of my father. Animal Tamer had had a special reflection at his great grandfather's deathbed; that now great grandfather was a spirit who could go everywhere and would always be with us. We never hinted at that, Animal Tamer is a self-made philosopher. Upon this insight, Animal Tamer waved the sandalwood incence of India made for great grandfather's benediction in his crossing.

An ancient Indian prayer runs: *May the dead and the living be lifted up together in soothing.* My father made his final transfer at Easter 2012. He left in blissful peace after a hard fight against his ill condition. He had been a constructor and a widely traveled businessman in his lifetime, named Bjarni after his ancestral Bear clan of a remote past who came to live in Norway and later Iceland. During the course of his eight year's of grim diabetes, he had lost both his legs and had had a stroke that left him lame and speechless--conditions he coped with magnanimously.

At the same time, he had had to deal with one medical professional's unfair conduct.

Such passing of a loved one begs questions of redefining what it means to be human within the context of one's present life. And, how life and death are seen in the modern outlook of things. Performing in society, measuring value in terms of money, estate, or high-tech gear and gadgets, being the ultimate focus; death as the most natural, unavoidable and certain of human realities, becomes alienated. Thus, a lost connection to the sacredness of life and death diminishes the dignity and rights of those terminally ill and dying and paves way for their exploitation.

When I left for Varanasi five months later, I had not yet had a dream of my father walking or talking, something that puzzled me being the dreamer I am; I was stuck.

# Knocking on Heaven's Door

When I was leaving for Varanasi, Animal Tamer confided in me that last night before going to bed, he had seen that turquoise Buddha statue in the living room *move. He opened his eyes and turned his head*, he said. Bought in Westmount in Montréal Canada, it had been with his family for several years. Both while living there during Animal Tamer's first years of life and later after crossing the Atlantic Ocean to live in Iceland some time ago.

I had long been knocking on Heaven's door when in the Summer of 2012, a pretty floral cotton scarf at a market shop came into my possession. It was made by Shiva design in India and had even been given a special name: written in one corner was TRANSFER. The time had come to fulfill a lifelong dream of paying Kashi a visit--Shiva's abode in the world. A visit to the oldest living city in the world, the City of Light on the banks of the Ganges--the River of Gods and the River of Time. The eternal city of transfer between worlds where death is in a leading role and many are cremated daily, believing that Mother Ganga will clean away their sins and cross them over to the great Hereafter. Or, for the living, taking a sacred dip in Her holy waters and being purified, washing away many a lifetime of sins.

Spirituality pulsates at the river ghats with Kashi watching times and trends coming and going. Once expiring here, Kashi offers *moksha* (liberation from the cycle of birth and death), making the city the hub of the Hindu universe. A Borderland. Truly a *thin* place.

Not long afterwards, I opted for a ticket to India and plans were on their way for the dream journey of a lifetime. I was given a new watch, ticking to an ancient time and a new future. It made me wonder if our dreaming is but a swift movement in space? What about this upcoming journey, I said to my son who drove me to Kelfavik international airport on my way London-Delhi-Varanasi, who had handed me the watch--a birthday present from my older psychic sister Stulla. He just smiled in his gentle manner looking excited about his mother's new beginnings.

I have always been a dreamer and began noting my dreams down at a young age. This lifelong interest in dreams was also at the back of my mind, wanting to learn more about the Indian dream heritage and compare it to our Icelandic one; I had eventually even set up a crosscultural research centre--*Skuggsja Dream Centre*. (*Skuggsja* is an old Icelandic word meaning mirror). Interest is and always has been strong in the meaning of dreams in India as it has been in Iceland together with interest in the great Hereafter. About two thirds of our Icelandic population believe in life after death, a different comsology, yes, to the one of Hinduism, nevertheless a similar belief in the continuum of consciousness and in the possibility of the continued evolution of the soul.

Dream symbolism and dream and sleep narratives abound in both Indian and Icelandic language and literature and are placed between dream and reality--they offer a means to move between different levels of reality. Or, as the Taittiriya Uphanishad states:

*The Spirit of man*
*has two dwellings:*
*this world and the world beyond.*
*There is also a third-dwelling place:*
*the land of sleep and dreams.*

When reaching London, my daughter and I spend the Autumn Equinox walking around Hampstead Heath in bright and brisk weather with the city at our footsteps and glimpsing a grey-blue Thames river. We blend in and sky gaze with a crowd on the hilltop. Then we walk into Hampstead Village where we pass John Keats house, his *Ode to a Nightingale,* comes to mind as it bears great resemblance to some verses from the *Rig Veda,* one of the oldest forest books of the so-called Indian forest writers who many lived in the eternal city of Kashi and wrote on birch-bark. Kashi's oldest name is blissful forest, *Anandakhan.*

Not only Keats, but many other poets, Shakespeare in *A Midsummer Night's dream*, Shelly in *Skylark*, and Coleridge in *Kubhla Khan*, were under a strong Indian influence in their dreamlike writing. They all speak of the immortal bird. His name is *Garuda* in Indian religious literature, the vehicle of Grandsire Brahma. Might he still be around? The threefold Pantheon or Godhead in Hinduism is Shiva the life preserver and destroyer, Vishnu the protector, and Brahma the creator--later I learn about the fourth, Mahesh.

Sleeping in the vicinity of Hampstead Heath before my London-Delhi flight, I have a dream of a green olive snake. He looks me softly in the eyes and with that I wake up in awe over how long he is and how many curves he has. I speculate on what space and time he comes from? He is at least too foreign for Hampstead Heath.

# In the Skies and on a Jet Plane

As I drive back home after seeing to our grandparents old house by the eastside of our fjord before embarking on my India journey, I notice a peculiar column of white-grey in the western skies, looking like a timble-shaped octagonal cylinder. It startles me as it reminds of a jyotir, a Shiva lingam. And in the evening news I hear of a meterior falling today. How mysterious. Well, one can read signs and symbols everywhere, or not.

In the British Airways plane on my way London-Delhi, flight 257, I have an aile seat at 44C with an empty midseat in this outsold plane. A Hinduwoman, presumably in her late fifties, sits in the window seat at 44A, clad in a marooni colored silk sari and brocades, wearing much gold jewellery. (Did I mention Kashi is the silk and brocade city of the world?) She speaks little English and bears the name of a famous citar player but plays to a different drum. We chat a bit and when asking about religion, if she is a Shiva devotee, (she has the Shiva dot painted on her forehead), she replies with a yes, but Mahesh. I wonder what she means and ask her about Maharisi Mahesh (the yogi of the Beatles) to which she just nods and smiles but with a waving hand. What does she really mean?

Dharma and karma; am I going here to get my karma in order? What is happening anyway and why am I after all going to Kashi? All I know is that fairness of conduct (*dharma*) follows one like a faithful dog throughout life, and that love is all there is--*Baba nam kevalam*. I also know that my mind drifts a lot like with the rest of people.

I help my travel companion fill in the landing form and bend over the empty seat to do that. She really does not need fill it in, I think, an Indian citizen of Punjab--former Panchand--the green state. Perhaps she has got mixed up after three months in the West. Punjab is one of the first areas in ancient India to be densely populated due to its fertile soil. This entrance to India is at the crossroads of East and West; the ancient multi-cultural city of Taxila was for instance located here and became a great seat of learning for Hindus and Buddhists alike. Greeks, Afghans, Persians, Indians, Pakistanis, all have fought for dominance.

It is easy to get mixed up on identity after all the twists and turns here in this land of five rivers and a presumed cradle of civilization in the Indus valley. I wonder who has not fought over it. The sages perhaps? Its Sivalik mountains and Himalachand bear witness to the lives of many sages, holy men and women--sadhus and sannyasis--from ages past and present. Nearby Jammu is the birthplace of Cowherd Krishna (a disguised Master of war and a God for the matter) of the epic *Mahabharata* with its ethical theme of action against non-action when dharma is threatened in the world.

Later I learn that *Mahesh* is an old name for the Lord mentioned in the Mahabharata and its *Bhagavad Gita* which

I first read as a teenager. I had got it from a bookstore of Russian Jews who had fled the Nazis and ran their bookstore of classical literature and internationally published religious texts next door to my home. Mahesh is often depicted as the fourth in the Godhead. What fellowship. A seat booked for someone at 44B who never turned up?

Together with the transfer of information in the modern world, we have the age-old concept of a transfer between states of consciousness towards liberation in our waking and dreaming experiences so well described in India's most famous Gita. On the transfer and the boat for crossing, the Bhagavad Gita runs:

*He who desires to cross the painful ocean of worldy life,*
*which is full of the crocodiles of lust, anger, greed, and infatuation,*
*should catch hold of the Bhagavad Gita*
*which has the disciplines of action,*
*devotion and wisdom as its oars.*
*It will easily take him to the land of liberation (Nirvana).*

Is there a message on my phone? I can only answer with OM. Mine does not work normally on the textboard but I know how to send an OM reply. At home they'll know all is well with me when they receive the OM. Yeah; a flying boat aka a jet plane is transferring me to Kashi and much transfer of information is going on all the time as we fly thru a whole matrix of crossing particles in a wireless world. We never seem to give it much thought or bother so long as the gear and gadgets work. If we had ultra vision, would we see these crossing particles of crystal transmitters as light lights? Or dark lights? Hindus believe Lord Shiva to rule the mineral kingdom, hence much Shiva power in the quartz crystals at the base of our modern technology.

OM for AMEN. Hey fellows, Hindu woman and Mahesh, I am very grateful for your company.

# India is Olive and Ganga is Milky

Sunrise over Delhi, a beige and orange line against a catching black background. At Delhi airport, the atmosphere is gentle and not so tenuous as is the usual airport experience. My first entrance to India is an encounter with the animal kingdom. Attention is drawn to the fact that animals are guardians of India and that they sleep and dream too! Decorations on walls, sculptures and paintings with a poster saying: *Wild dreams. A snail can sleep for three days*! A text to one side of huge statues of a grown elephant and a baby one reads: *Ganesha for new beginnings, wisdom and success.*

A large blue-grey dove flies in straight line over my head to the front daylit windowposts. Or is this a dove? Looks quite a character. Salute, Suryasand; I bow to thee Sun in all your majestic glory still struggling with the appropriate mudras.

Flying Kashi in broad daylight over olive India. Rivers bend and bristle. Ganga looks like a milkyway in this olive land. I hardly believe my own eyes, I never expected to have Ganges as a sweet sister enroute Varanasi. Mother Ganga flows a long way from the Gangroti glacier in the high Himalayas. Looks a living phantom from air, an endless flow of milk. And not surprisingly, they say she flows from a cow's mouth in those majestic far Himalayan pavillions. Two thirds of the population are located on Her banks. A giver of life and a harbinger of death. Ancient Kashi is ideally placed to greet the rising sun over the holy river.

Into the far mist ahead, Ganga stretches. Never disappears entirely but becomes ever more magical almost lofty towards a thin place at the far horizon by the Bay of Bengal where the white tiger abides. Silverballs beam from the ground, they look like silver lights against the ivory and olive background. As the plane lowers for landing on the outskirts of Kashi, one sees they are indeed electrical lights from huts and larger houses alike.

# A Forest City hosts a Lingam

Kashi is a grove, an ancient grove of long gone trees. This worldly abode of Shiva and his beloved consort Parvati is a forest of bliss. A forest city based in a grove on the Ganga banks. A sacred complex and a microcosm of Indian civilization hosting the most revered jyotir or lingam of all--the age-old Viswanath. Has the lingam emerged from the crust of the Earth and been flashed towards the sky? Or is the jyotir a meteor that once fell to Earth?

Hundreds of shrines and temples are scattered all over the city along with a myriad of stalls selling silks and brocades; ghat by ghat down by the river. However, the city is built around its main attraction, the Golden Temple thus named because of its guilded spire where the jyotir is placed, one Kashi Vishwanath is the ruling deity here--a form of Lod Shiva. A centre of worship, the most sacred of all, with pilgrims, mostly devoted Hindus, streaming in daily from all over India.

The Golden Temple was raised by the queen of Indore in the late 18th century after one of those raids on Kashi that ruined the city. There have been countless ruins and countless rebirths of the City of Light throughout history. This city truly is a sadhu and a sannyasi, a city of much devotion and learning whatever the earthly scenery. No wonder it hosts India's number one university, Banares Hindu University; BHU.

Imagine entering a medieval rag-tag city of either low crumbling or tall scewed buildings of incoherent designs almost falling down upon you with its many galis or streets. Old Varanasi's layout is like a matrix of a few broad galis surrounding the Golden Temple with adjoining narrow galis inside the layout eventually leading to the Temple centre. The narrow galis hustle and bustle with people coming and going day in and day out, of animals coming and going, of bikes coming and going. At first glance, this city of trade and trading looks pretty chaotic. It reminds of medieval towns in Europe like in Italy or even England, Bradford - upon - Avon being a good example. A magical city and not for the faint-hearted. Kashi is so much taller, louder, more chaotic than any city I've visited, with the worst ever traffic of cars and motorbikes blowing their horns every second. Then there are the cows...

# Monu or Moon Stay

Now I have reached not only Kashi but Monu, my abode while here. Monu for moon, and needless to say, the guesthouse stands at a crossroads. Perhaps one night I shall go out, lay myself down at the crossroads and envision what there is to come as was the old custom in our Nordic folklore with moongazing and prophezising.

Monu is located on the outskirts of the Golden Temple in a medieval looking narrow gali named Kalika gali due to the nearby Kali Temple. Actually Goddess Kali stamped Her in my first night with a loudly playing *A black magic woman* as Kashi's - or should I say Kali's - popculture is alive and thriving every night at Yogi Lodge and its Oasis restaurant across from here.

I sleep beneath a heaven of earthly coloured yantras and mantras in yellow, green, blue and violet where the air conditoner is the central condensed dot of universal bliss. My sense perceptions are in for a twist, it feels like being in the hypnagogic state between wake and sleep with flickering shapes every time I lie down. No hallucinations though. Some of my dreams overlap the boundaries of my sleep making me wonder if I'm awake or dreaming; I experience multiple levels of awareness in the wake and reflective awareness in dreaming from the start. I fly in a dream and feel flying the next day too. Not spaced out or anything. My dreams are vivid and some lucid ones take me to transpersonal spheres in color where I encounter personalized figures some resembling Wisdom Devi Sarasvati playing her vina all dressed in white, and Beauty and Wealth Devi Lakshmi with a coral complexion floating on a lotus.

This yantric-mantric room is my room at Monu, decorated according to visions of the owner Madhav. The long gone beloved Bindu Madhav Temple resurfacing in a vision of a reborn geometrician? Madhav or *Mad Honey* as he calls himself is my landlord. He saw this all in his mind, he explains. All the guesthouse is now painted in these colors and shapes and so are its seven rooms. Mine is number five. Mad Honey points proud to a picture of the Golden Temple above the window and another to the side: here we have Kashi Viswanath of the Golden Temple, Lord Shiva gazing with a garland of flowers and a green snake around his blue neck. And, from my window, opposite Monu, I see an elegant small white Shiva Temple with a black flag at the top.

I have a dream this first night of my grandparents' cottage. I always loved it there. Now the house is empty of all furniture and the rooms look very much like the rooms here at Monu. I spot a single desk in the middle of the living room. On it there are some papers and a "Kristinn Jonsson" signs them. With that I wake up, the name has a peaceful ring to it. *Kristinn* means one who is devoted to the Christ.

# Dust and Stars at Burningghat

Being made of stardust, to dust and stars we shall return.
And be reborn? Death welcomed me already the first day
on my way through Kashi's mainstreet, Vishwanath gali,
when we saw a dead body all wrapped up and tied down
on barrows being carried through the crowds and traffic to
the Burningghat--the Jewelledghat or Manikarnikaghat--
the sanctuary of death with its ceaselessly smoking funeral
pyres around the clock. A stone, the quartz crystal, is at the
centre of modern technology such as in our microchips.
Manikarnika is where Shiva lost His crest stone *mani* and
Parvati her earring *karnika*.

No surprise that the Lord of the mineral kingdom rules
the fire for the cremation of bodies and the eventual blend of
elements. With the River of Gods--Ganga Devi--engulfing
the remains, chests for males and hips for females; these
bodyparts burn slowest. A normal cremation takes about
two to three hours. A sacred fire burning for ages is said to
light the cremation pyres bestowing blessings for a good life
and a good death. Death among living is a daily sight on the
streets of Kashi with a couple of hundred being burnt at that
ghat every day and carried through the galis.

Not long after, I see another body followed by many relatives. But is this body dead or still dying, I wonder. The halfsitting corpse in the open vehicle stares me softly in the eye; m*ay sorrow end in peace.* Sweet death in a city advertised as a city of death. Probably no city on the planet would get that description or be proclaimed as the true remover of sin that many believe Kashi to be. Earlier reflecting on British poets under Indian influence such as Keats, one verse from his masterpiece on the mystery of mortality and death *Ode to a nightingale* runs:

*Darkling I listen; and, for many a time*
*I have been half in love with easeful Death,*
*Call'd him soft names in many a mused rhyme,*
*To take into the air my quiet breath.*

Who knows wither? Like falling asleep, a change in consciousness takes place as you loose consciousness and transfer to another consiousness, or what? Dreaming being an example everyone knows, dying another everyone shall face. And needless to say, most of the time we take our transfers for granted and without thinking.

Overall there exists a rich in-depth perception of changes of consciousness and dreams in India. Scholars speak of a multiplicity of approaches that reflect the richness of the dream tradition with readiness to incorporate dreams at many levels of life and any system of thought. A well-known symbolic dream of snakes relates to Manikarnika. Once, a famous sadhu walked along the banks of the Ganga and saw two snakes playing beside the Burningghat. In the following night, he saw a dream of his guru Baba Nagannath who told him to establish *an akhara* at the exact site where the snakes had been playing. Not long afterwards, the place became an akhara, a famous wrestling place for training spiritual warriors.

# Big-Hearted Ganesha

In Indian mythology, the elephant is revered as an absolutely precious creature to be protected and cared for and takes many forms as the vehicle of the gods. In the form of Ganesha, he is the popular ubiquitos deity of new beginnings, wisdom and success. A gentle and dignified giant who serves as a synthesis of Hinduism.

Last night, I had a dream vision of a newly born baby elephant who gazes at me as he lies on the ground. With strong footing, he raises himself up and willingly starts to carry heavy burdens. His devoted heart is big and pure. (An elephant's heart weighs around twenty to fourty kilos and beats about thirty times a minute). Suddenly he turns tiny and gets into the iris of my left eye...

Strolling now down the Kalika gali towards Ganga out in the open plane of Vishwanath gali. Well, if you can call this main street open! Tons of people, one large moving multicultural and multireligious mob engulfs Vishwanath every single day. Most of them Hindus though, it seems. A young guide, one Vinay Singh accompanies me to the most popular ghat where the fire cermony takes place every night just across from the Golden Temple. This ghat goes by the name *Dashaswamedhghat* and is the ancient entrance of Lord Brahma on a *swamedh* or a horse to Mother Ganga where he made a ten (das) horses sacrifice to Lord Shiva and the holy river.

The sacred river is at our footsteps as we cautiously move on sliding stonesteps down to the banks with old scewed buildings overlooking in various shapes, styles and colors. Ganga looks very much like a living being, a mesmerizing force having a say in everything. Thought I would have peace and quiet down here but alas no. The beggars are out and young mothers with infants scream for milk. Nothing is enough, and few tourists or locals give anything at all. I give some rupees but must learn the real meaning of this life style. Where is the serenity and holiness? I now think Kashi has lost it, but hey. Life is colorful.

On my way back, I pay a visit to the Santosh Silk House and Babú in a side gali close to Vishwanath. I bought no silk this time but a soft cotton bag decorated with Ganesha prints. Yeah; the elephant God Ganesha is alive and well with shrines and temples dedicated to him all over the place. I even carry Him myself as an amulet, a necklace I happened to come upon at a beauty saloon last Summer.

Actress Goldie Hawn is a regular customer at Babú's, her first visit was in 1982 when Babú had just bought the shop after having won the state lottery. Now he is in his sixties but had earlier been a guide and a boatman like so many men here in their younger days. Babú is a Shiva devotee who paints the Shiva mantra on his forehead every morning and has done so over the past twenty three years. He goes to the

Golden Temple daily for chanting mantras for a couple of hours--reciting jaap hundred and eight times--in the late afternoon. Actually, he looks like a laughing Buddha.

Next I pay a visit to still another silk merchant, or should I say a seventh generation weaver? A true son of Kashi like all his ancestral family in the silk trade. Kabir, the great weaver of Kashi during medieval times and poet-sage comes to mind. This guy now moves my heart and I find tears coming to flood from deep within my soul. Life moves in mysterious ways, no denying that. Varanasi born and comes from a long line of weavers back six to seven generations. This is Ramesh the weaver, a wannabe politician. One good spokesman, I notice at our first encounter. Ramesh runs his father's shop next door, I met him already the first day of my stay at Monu.

He says I walk fast and talk fast, probably true, I want to fly and prefer silence to small talk. Then he says I never forget a face or a name, probably true as well, my profession as a psychotherapist has trained my eye and ear.

# End Dimension of the Material Universe

Today I notice parties of sadhus in the galis. Is something happening today or what? And later on, I see about fourty to fifty of them bathing down at Dashaswamedh, looking very happy. I wonder about Babaji. The people I have asked about Babaji whom Yogananda spoke of in his *Autobiography of a Yogi* say there are so many Babas or Babajis and turn mysterious. They say the real sadhus come from the mountains and occasionally stay for eight to ten days in Kashi and do not let anyone know; that they mingle without people realizing.

An older sadhu in a marooni cloth sits meditating opposite Ramesh's shop this morning when I come out. A bird sang last night near my window, his high pitched song was full of hope and reminded me of our Newton at home, our green Indian ring neck. Several dimensions unite here in Kashi, they say, the universal and creative dimension, the preserving dimension, and the end dimension of the material universe. And, in this oldest city on the planet, time turns the tide with Lord Vishnu's--the Great Developer's--mount Bird Garuda tuning in. Many people here seem to be on a pilgrimage of nonexistence with no need for fear of the void or to fill the void with material gains. The eyes of the world are like blind to them.

Dreaming is vivid and effortless, it feels like I keep moving through layers and layers of consciousness and I encounter celestial spheres. I had a dream vision last night, I was sitting on a lotus flower with a family of celestial beings surrounding. Then I felt like levitating in air and I made a visit to a city in the sky. Afterwards back to bed at Monu, I kept asking myself if this was IT? That the real Kashi is a celestial city above the city, hence her name the City of Light?

Origins of reigning dynasties, or epoch sketches, are found in Kashi's written history with accounts of pilgrimages and sacred rites. Laying on the highway of trade and exchange via the Ganges, Kashi early became a revered place of learning--hosting not only a university but several schools of thought--wherefrom much spiritual knowledge radiated. History shows the city served as a great resonator in antiquity and medieval times of the Babylonian, Syrian, Egyptian, Arabian, Ephesian, Chinese and Indian cultures. Today, this meeting point between Hinduism, Buddhism, Jainism, Jewism, Christianity and Muslim reflects an interesting mix, now with a Western twist. I just love the mix and the twist!

When going in for dinner at Ganga Fuji Restaurant, the owner Kailash told me the story of the four names of the city. First there was Anandakhan for a gentle and lovely forest at the river where sadhus came for worship and meditation. That's when Shiva came and nothing of human habitat existed. He named it Kashi, the City of Light. Later after Vasco da Gama had sailed to India, the British came. They used it for harbour for the East India Company and the port became known as Banares. Indians from all over started to flock early for prayers and devotion. The latest name Varanasi is a combination of the two ghats Assighat and Varunaghat with big bridges to both sides, one over the Ganges and the other over adjacent river Varuna. Monday is Shiva day and it is on one such day that I learn from Kailash the four names of this magical city. Incidentally his name is the one of mount Kailash which is claimed in religious texts to be Shiva's eternal abode in the Himalayas.

Sleep was not too good last night except for a few hours late into night and early morning. It's a beautiful warm day as I sit down on the roof top of the Brown Bread Bakery having a late breakfast. Good view over Old Varanasi and towards Ganga. Would the goats and sheep down there be out and about? I must admit the sheep down at Dashaswamedh have taken me by surprise. Not unlike the English ones, and I never expected them here anyway. Tons of mosquitos are now at the other side of the net dying for a bite. I am still half fasting and I do not like suckers of any kind anyhow. The midges at home always want a bite too.

Quickly I finish the banana pancakes and lemon tea to go for some sightseeing towards the market at *Baba Black Sheep*. Some real good shops are around, and the church of St. Thomas in stark yellow and white, towers over the roundabout in sharp contrast to everything else. Still a part of it all. A city of contrasts for sure. But I like this Baba Black Sheep. It rings to the inner child, a black sheep with the added Baba makes all the difference and feels welcoming.

# Vishwanath or the Man Himself?

On my way from Baba Black Sheep down Vishwanath gali, I pass one of the four entrances to the Golden Temple with heavy police guard. Devotees are pouring in. I head for the Dashaswamedh and Ganga at noon like I do daily and notice about ten to twelve sadhus sitting in two straight lines to my right near the ghat's entrance. What is happening here today? All wearing orange cloth and noone tries to speak to me or ask for money as is the custom with so many fake sadhus. A few raise their right hand in a gesture of blessing.

There is an odd one out, ageless and motionless in the back row closest to the ghat, he sits in a lotus posture with eyes wide open. Just wears his breechcloth. A strongly built man and taller than most men around. His long black hair is taken up in a large Shiva knot at the crown with locks rolling down and the Shiva mantra painted on his forehead. He looks from another dimension and an eternal one. And it suddenly strikes me that he looks like an exact replica of the pictured Shiva in my room at Monu (in the picture from the Golden Temple). Kashi Vishwanath in person? After I return from my noon prayers at Ganga, He is still there but when returning later after some afternoon tea with Babú,

He is here no more but the remaining sadhus nodd friendly and raise hands; great bonding skills, I feel.

The deep psychology encountered in the evolution of ideas I've been reading about in the *Footfalls of Indian History* by the Irish lady Margaret Noble is quite intriguing and much to the point. Initially, Margaret Noble came to India and worked as a teacher. She turned Hindu and was given the name sister Nivedita, a devotee of Swami Vivekananda who had been a disciple of that well-known 19th century Bengali born mystic Ramakrishna at the famous Dakshineswar Kali Temple near Kolkata. Ramakrishna followed a non-dualistic approach rooted not only in Hindu, but in Muslim and Christian traditions as well: *All paths lead to same God*.

According to sister Nivedita, the more modern Hindu gods are subjective and their sphere is in the soul, their power that of high ideals. They belong to a different class from that of the old nature-gods. Furthermore, the old gods--Indra, Agni, Yama, and Varuna--represented external forces. The old gods had been cosmic and irresistible in their might, glorious and lovable, but not of the Within. Instead they had been supremely objective. The blisterous days of storm, fire and forest worships once far behind, goddesses such as Kali, Puskara and Savitri, became the sheer force of the spiritual ideal that lived on in ancient India. The Devi as Durga or Parvati belonging almost unconsciously to the coming era of subjective soul-staying faiths. Hence, the religious faculty of humanity, sister Nivedita concludes, is as much feminine as masculine. Within this frame of thought, Shiva is seen as the subtle poetic conception of the great monk throned on the snow, lost in eternal meditation. And, in the prayer to Rudra, the great Lord Shiva is established finally as the light of knowledge within the soul; Rudra had used to be the God of wind and storm and hunt.

The prayer to Rudra from the Rig Veda was translated in the late 19th century by Swami Vivekananda. He was the first yoga master to enter the USA and speak at the Parliament of World Religions in Chicago in 1893 and introduce yoga and meditation to the West:

*From unreal*
*Lead us to the Real*
*Reach us through and*
*through our self.*
*And ever more protect us*
*Oh Thou Terrible! –*
*From ignorance,*
*By Thy sweet compassionate face!*

# Fire Ceremony and Tarakeshwara

Death holds a sacred place in Kashi, is welcomed, not feared. The greatest holy power of Kashi is the power of bestowing liberation on the devoted, *Moksha* or *Mukti*. Devotees believe death in Kashi is death transformed and gives liberation. May the eternal ferryman--Shiva in the form of Tarakeshwara--guarantee father's safe crossing. Dusk descending, I am attending the fire ceremony this evening when Ganga Aarti is being performed. At this ancient ritual of Agni Puja, a group of priests makes a dedication through fire to Lord Shiva, River Ganga, Surya the Sun, Agni the Fire, and the whole universe.

I deeply feel I've come to this great venue to bid my last farewell to my deceased father on his final transfer. First we had had the traditional Christian funeral back home, now the time has come for a Hindu ceremony celebrating his death, life and bygone days of his somewhat Hindu upbringing at the far northern shores. His mother had been one of the first disciples of yoga in Iceland. Of Kriya yoga to be specific. The Taraka mantra, or the ferryboat mantra, the mantra of the final transfer, is whispered in the ear of the dying by Shiva, the teacher at death's door. The mantra of liberation. May father's passage be blissful.

Several devotees have come tonight from all over India attending the fire ceremony in the company of their well-known gurus. I light a candle where I stand high up on the side steps to the left with a good view of all the ceremonial proceedings. I am in the wonderful company of a large family from the Heart of India - Madhya Pradesh - wherefrom the queen of Indore came to establish the Golden Temple of Vishwanath in the 18th century. Two elderly couples and a few younger devotees on their long awaited pilgrimage now bestow flowers upon me. One of the older ladies paints a mantra on my forehead as they sing praise.

Much aarti is going on downstairs at the main platform and the cermonial fires stretch towards heaven together with shimmering lights of puja on the dark and tranquil Ganga full of boats and more devotees. The gurus sit upstairs above the platform where the orchestra is playing. My fellows keep waving their beloved gurus up there, praying, dancing and shouting Jai Shiva, Om Shanti. I dance too, then sit down with my eyes closed, feeling the vibe of it all. Suddenly tears spring forth from the depths of my soul and I cry softly. Fire has touched me. These sweet tears shooth my grieving heart; full of trust in the eternal ferryman and his mantra whispered to the ones in transfer, I let father go. May the River of Time caress him forth in a final embrace with the wheel of dharma.

As the tide of Time is turned once more in a Brahmaloka universe containing all of our Earth and other worlds, we embark on a new future. Intuitively I feel that Animal Tamer shall come here onc day to pay respects and be touched by Fire. So it says in Katha Uphanishad:

*Listen. That Fire which is the means*
*of attaining the Infinite Worlds,*
*and is also their foundation,*
*is hidden in the sacred place of the heart.*

The young girl and wannabe-guide I met few days ago down by Dasaswamedh, taps me on the shoulder: My friend. You are crying?

# Animal Lords

A brand sunny day it is. The dog barks at dawn as usual and the bird chirps in tune as they celebrate the rise of a glorious morning sun. From my window, I hear light feet hurry towards Ganga for bathing and praying. In the night, I had a dream of my old workplace at the hospital and of some former colleagues at Akureyri university. Suddenly a young man appeared and offered me help with some papers. The dream changed and I was now visiting an old house that once beleonged to my uncle where I met up with my daughter. My uncle used to be the head of police and the house had been a police station at one time.

(Police are everywhere in this City of Light and I have been wondering why. One answer is that the police guard relics around the clock all over Hindus' holiest city).

I woke up and contemplated on the dream, then slept again and now I saw a small thin half-cuddled up snake (or a fish) on a disc in shallow water raise his head towards me. I was astonished at the sight and when I examined further, I saw him look at me from one side with a long eye. This eye was very much alive but looking dead! It struck me when I looked at his neck if this neck was a tiny elephant's neck, or a snake's neck perhaps? At least, no ordinary fish's neck.

On my morning stroll towards Baba Black Sheep, something magical happened. I met young Lala who works in one of the family shops around and he offered to accompany me on the walk and take me to a side gali where people were preparing a special celebration for Lord Ganesha tonight. And here I met the largest Ganesha statue in all Kashi now decorated with flowers but little waterflow in His plate so I remarked that perhaps His Lordship needed more water! A salutation: Jai Ganesha.

From where I went down through a ghat with extraordinary views over Ganga. It was noon already, my favorite time of saluting the River of Time because of the quietude and lack of crowds at that particular hour. Flowing like a liquidated beige diamond with blue streaks and of a vibrant quality. To my right, I could see the Hanuman Temple with His figure in red--this Remover of Sorrow--and to the left there was the ancient temple to Nandi--the bull of Shiva and His vehicle in the world. Nandi's statues are the ones that have most often survived destruction in times of trouble in Kashi's often violent history. And, down here at the Nandi temple, is where the evening aartis are being held when water overflows the ground level temples where the fire ceremony normally takes place.

Down by the river, brown-red monkeys are flying all about, they are of the same type but of various sizes and ages. In the Nandi temple, the tallest and longest of them goes for my white scarf once bought on the streets of Paris, sold to me as pashmati turning out viscose. Let's say it's a good street scarf to be torn at by a teasing temple monkey. *No, I am not giving you the scarf,* monkey. Clearly he likes it more than an empty plastic soda bottle lying on the temple floor. Some tuc of war until I and scarf break free. It turns out to be of great utility during my whole stay in Kashi. Hindu friends call it my white saari and find it pretty.

Upon leaving, I cross an elegant tall white building with balconies near the river bank. Many beautiful buildings, people's homes at the Ganga, are located on this side of the river. Quite a walk this was, meeting up with Ganesha, Hanuman and Nandi in one stroll and finding real houses full of people, not decaying houses. But hey, people live in all the houses, decaying or what; after all, the city must house five millions.

# Business Around the Clock

The guides have told me of the custom of cheating and exploiting tourists. Probably very true but so far I've been lucky. I suspect them to tease people also like the monkeys do. This culture is interestingly twisted between the material and the spiritual. Animal Tamer says we stem from monkeys and birds from dinosaurs and is not sure of God, if there is one or ever was, and that Santa may be a handy fabrication.

Selling and buying is the real theme of material Kashi with myriad of shops and stalls in old Varanasi open long hours, most honest but some now dealing in drugs at the back. And once your money is gone noone will bother, say the locals, as happens with some of the young folk coming here for drugs. The shop and market system operates between the business people as a huge newtwork where each supports another and often a wealthy benefactor operates behind the scenes. I had learned about a similar network in Egypt during my visit there with my son in 1999. Families are large with next of kin and more distant relatives and friends knit in a tight social network in which people help each other out.

Religion is alive and thriving and woven into the fabric of a fixed routine around the clock, keeping the ghats naturally busy with Ganga Devi and the Golden Temple as the sacred hubs of life. Many celebrations take place here every month, not to mention kiirtan and puja at dawn and aarti at night. Recently, awareness is being raised towards the purification of Ganga against the pollution of modern lifestyle. One effort is the *Black Kashi Project* where people from all wards of life unite to keep the river free of chemicals and garbage, fighting at same time for an increased waterflow which has become broken because of faraway dams. Some days, I can easily see the almost empty shore at the other side when the river has a narrow flow. I had always imagined river Ganga so wide, a broad pathway for so many things on heaven and earth. And that actually is her natural style and always was.

Transfer in time through the river between worlds is an ongoing process in Kashi. What really happens in the passage is far from understood though. But so be this timeless flow in time and space. Transfer happens every second every day in some way or other, phoning from India to Iceland is an example, an expensive one for the matter. Particles swirl in a vast matrix. Fuel for economy and money to many. Be they monkeys or what.

# Lessons from Monu

*What is the meaning of your name Monu*, I ask the young man, son of my landlord. *It's mono like in monostereo*, he laughs, and looks at his father Madhav who gave him his Monu nickname. *I have another name for school*, he says. Younger people do not necessarily get old sanskrit names any more as was the old custom, rather something modern such as from technology. But Monu in sanskrit means moon so I am truly at Moon House with Shiva having a crescent moon in His hair in my room number five.

Monu tells me all about his education, work, future plans and work ethic wanting to be self-employed and run his own business. Very modern and youthful thinking. Soon twenty-seven and getting married, he holds a Master's degree of English literature from Gandhi university in 2008. Earlier he had gained a degree in music from BHU, holds a diploma in French too and now works on becoming a qualified tourist guide. Quite a philosophical mind, I notice. Believes barriers are dividing people and that hey arise in the mind. *Only one god*, he says. *Loves all religions; man should seek God within, no need to go to the Temple. Many are greedy and go there to ask God to give them something. Like going in a shop wanting something*, he proclaims. *Then when they don't need Him, they forget to worship and pray.* Quite an outlook spoken from an intelligent innocent, I feel.

Reminds me of Krishnamurti's teaching whom I actually had listened to in Saanen in Switzerland in the early eighties. Amitir at Yogi Lodge is Monu's nephew and went to the Krishnamurti school here in Varanasi and stayed for over ten years. He has fostered Monu with Madhav and his wife Indu and Monu's older sibling sister and psychologist. Today is a good day, Monu tells me, he is having his new lab computer for the tourist guide training programme, and explains he is going for a month and away on Monday and will see less of me for the time I have left of my stay at Monu.

These lessons now conclude my happy and sunny Saturday at Varanasi with the great architect and psychologist watching over it all.

# Daily Bread and Yoga

Sunday has shown it's benign face and I am well rested. Finally, a normal sleep over a full night. Now just having a peaceful Sunday morning. I am going to Ganga Fuji for Banana Lassi and some good lemon tea. A wonderful start of the day that agrees with my stomach.

Next, I find myself walking down to the ghat at noon. Should the beggar woman be there with her son? I had met her already the first day, I must ask her about the infant. Vinay says her husband was a soldier but fell ill and is out of work. There are many beggars here at Dashaswamedh every day, a real trade for livelihood, I suppose, and I fear people are being exploited on both sides.

On my way to the ghat, I meet a middle-aged sadhu with beard not long though, dark-haired in a dark-red marooni cloth. He greets me but says nothing. Once I reach the ghat, I notice a column by the security gate with information on the history of Dashaswamedh. As I have not noticed it earlier, I wonder if it has been there all along or put up now before the start of the *International Buddhist Conclave* this weekend? Anyhow, the reading explains quite well the true meaning of Dashaswamedh. It is at the same time the most popular ghat where all the action takes place. I shall go back to write down the entire text, the story of the horseghat moves my heart...

Last night, I had a dream in which I felt I could float in a beam of water over Kashi and take the city into my heart like one big complex. I felt I stood at the gate overlooking Ganga at the Nandi Temple and suddenly in the vision, the dreamscape changed and I was moved to my old room upstairs at grandma's. When looking around, the room is just as I had left it before leaving home at nineteen, and I feel content being here in this tranquil atmosphere of bygone days. Babaji comes to mind, my first lessons of Him took place here. (When my grandma (my dad's mum) Bjorg whom I am named after had got ill during the last year of life, I used to take care of her, help comb her long hair and bathe. What a blessing it had been and how much it helped me to cope when she eventually passed). This is one ultra-vivid impression of my room. Just step in and everything is the way it was.

Grandma had her long silver-hair in pleads and always wore the Icelandic costume on Sundays. A devoted Christian going to church every Sunday for mass and singing hymns but at the same time she was very broad minded towards religion and different ways of life; she was one of the first practitioners of yoga in Iceland. She practiced with friends from our hometown of Akureyri, some of whom had moved down south to the capital where she went reglulary to meet up with them to study yoga literature and meditate.

One of her yoga friends was teacher and author Adalbjorg Sigurdardottir, the wife of the first professor of theology at the University of Iceland, Haraldur Nielsson, who was well-known for his broad spiritual and religious emphases. Adalbjorg was a great dreamer from childhood onwards and records exist of her dreams from seven years of age. She later became a follower of Jiddu Krishnamurti who had broken free from traditional guruship and opted for a *find out yourself* psychological revolution and a radical change in society. Incidentally, my clinic in Reykjavik is based in a house in the city centre near the university run by the wife of Adalbjorg´s greatgrandson. Nothing intended really, only happens to be so.

During my adolescence years, I had my room on grandma's floor in our large house of twenty-three rooms by the townsquare. This was a world of my own with my spiritual books, some given me by dad, bought on his many travels in Europe, and journals from grandma on yoga, some on Babaji, the eternal yogi of the Himalayas. We often cooked vegetarian meals and drank herbal teas with drops of honey, something that took me time to take a liking to. A huge vegetable garden was at the back of our street where we could have vegetables as we liked. Then there was a huge potato garden and rhubarb growing too. A neighbour living at number five, even had a glasshouse where he grew strawberries.

Next to the gardens, a small brown bread bakery eventually opened by the Health Food Society, grandma being one of the founders. We loved the bread from them. The newly baked whole grain bread I now buy from the Brown Bread Bakery here, its smell and taste, reminds me of our daily bread when growing up and receiving my first yoga lessons in kriya yoga with simple breathing exercises and some basic asanas. A lifestyle not many were accustomed to at the time but in the long run of things, is well established now in our far Northern country.

My grandpa was a great family man with many friends and family from the North-West where he initially lived. And from the North-East, members of grandma's family came to stay for longer or shorter times. What a wonderful hub, and how much love and freedom we had as children growing up among all those good people in Akureyri town centre--many-hued as they were from all walks of life.

# A Dream of India

Daily, I used to read something in my room on the various paths of yoga be they karma yoga, raja yoga, gnani yoga, bhakti yoga, or hatha yoga, and from an early start of my reading, I developed a yearning for India. A dream of going there one day, even to work and do something good for the poor people because at this period in the sixties and seventies, one read about the poverty stricken nation and how it had been exploited for centuries by foreign powers and traders. I read about the father of a nation, Mahatma Gandhi whom all my folk at home loved and his dream of India as a free democratic state giving every man an opportunity to live a decent life. What an enormous effort he had made, and what achievement when India finally got independence in 1947.

Here in Kashi, this city of weaving fabric out of thread to make something pretty--a magical act indeed--I feel as much at home as at home. No wonder my dreams take me back to my roots as I had quite a strong weaving and somewhat unusual sewing experience while growing up. Cloth, texture of fabric, the feel of good quality, how well-tailored, are special sights to a trained eye. And it all started with grandma as she was one of the first qualified tailoresses in the country for the national costume. Initially, she had come from the far northeast countryside to learn the trade from grandpa's Danish brother-in-law. That's how they met at our house by the townsquare built by grandpa and his family at the turn of the 20th century.

Grandpa was twelve years her senior, a strict officer and the head of the social services in town, the title at the time was *a spokesman for the poor*. A very gentle and good grandpa to us children, no matter how strict and distant others saw him. Perhaps he took his public appearance after some of his British friends who had stayed with him and grandma in the house during the Second World War--officers who served at this northernmost post. Yes, Kashi – the ancient city of weaving - always was the magical dream. And a scarf indeed, woven and made in India and bought at an Icelandic market shop, served as the trigger for my long awaited visit to this oldest and holiest city on Earth.

Their son, my father, was the biggest baby ever born in Iceland in modern time. He held the record for decades to come according to the national register of midwives. He was born on 27 June 1929--on *Seven Sleepers Day*--and it so happened that later in his life, I graduated from both my BA-studies and Ph.d. in Psychology on his birthday.

# Who is Who?

The dog did not bark early this Sunday morning, perhaps he has been trained to stay silent on a Sunday? Instead a tiny antlord appeared in the eve. His bulk was white like porcelain and his many outstretched arms were ornated in red, yellow and gold and he wore a colorful headdress too. His materialisation appeared in the doorway to the bathroom. Earlier that afternoon, I had had an encounter with the first insect in the bathroom during my stay, whatever insect it was. It became the first and only insect that I destroyed while in India. When the antlord appeared, I asked pardon. Did this encounter happen in my dream or my wake, or was my wake but a dream within a dream?

Memories of the first encounter with my Ph.d. supervisor at Stirling university in Scotland are being brought back. When preparing for my research into language development, he gave me some materials to read, the first book and a must read, was one on the consciousness of ants! Further, my doctoral experiments into the decipherment of word meaning were based on medieval Grail-lore, and on that extraodinary work on the five styles of English, *the Five Clocks,* by Toronto professor, electric engineer and linguist Martin Joos. Quite a surreal work in style and time; tick-tock.

My other supervisors from within the field of experimental psychology have been equally unconditional however strict in their scientific endeavours. My Canadian supervisor for instance asked me out of the blue if I believed in reincarnation when I first met her! And my Icelandic supervisor for the undergraduate thesis into mystical and religious experience, kept showing me how his Indian master could make gold rings out of thin air! And kept praising his idol in science, parapsychologist par excellence Stanley Krippner, whom I later met at a costume ball in Berkeley dressed up as some vegetable at an event hosted by the International Association for the Study of Dreams; IASD. Like the experience with the antlord in the bathroom door, one never really knows who is who. Or, do we deep down?

# Encountering the Primal

Ramesh is taking me for a tour to the Inner City and New Varanasi. We shall visit BHU and the New Kashi Vishwanath Temple located on the university grounds, a beautiful plot given for its construction by Kashi Nareesh of the old guardian and raj family of Varanasi. It is around three when we leave Monu for a tuk-tuk that takes us through Old Varanasi's main street to New Varanasi. The difference is striking, broader streets--not messy.

The Temple stands on the university grounds and is quite beautiful. We head straigth for the Shiva lingam hall-- barefoot on marble. At the shrine there is this elderly Brahmin and a young woman serving the flow of water over the lingam. The Brahmin sits by the lingam's side to my right. I bow my head and say *namaste* and he gives me a beige clay dot on the forehead - some *vibuthi* - and then he reaches out to the lady for a garland of white flowers and puts over my head. It is quite surprising and Ramesh was amazed at it too.

I am very grateful for this experience and it took me to my dream of Saturday night. Because now in real wake, I saw clearly the cobra towering over the lingam and protecting it. And the eye that turned to me was strange to look at, it felt like a burst olive eye--almost dead--as in the dream.

The temple is a replica of the Old Vishwanath Temple, based on two grand floors and has a very tall spire wherefrom one can see the whole city of Varanasi. I was fascinated by the poster writings and the paintings with verses from the Gita and the Upanishads on the temple walls; a tranquil atmosphere once sitting down to contemplate. I also saw some elegant statues of female deities such as Durga and Lakshmi, and of male deities such as Vishnu and Hanuman. Spacious and elegant, the temple awakes feelings of simplicity and awe. Outside in the garden there was Nandi sheltered in wooden piles protected from the monsoons.

We spent quite some time on the balcony where a mother with her five children asked a photo to be taken of us by Ramesh. The gardens beneath are peaceful and students use to read here in the coolness of the trees. In a fleeting moment, I felt I saw the Shiva figure cast on a large tree...

I have asked Ramesh to write down for me the name of the Brahmin who was at the lingam shrine and gave me the white garland. Ramesh goes regularly to the temple and says this priest is a very high caste brahmin and known as such in society. Care is taken with water flowing over the lingam around the clock, concealing the energy of the times or the Primal. In a more symbolic form for the Primal is an artistic presentation of Shiva showering in the Ganga splashing water in all directions; time and space meet in blissful union. He is then *Kaal* or Time--both the destroyer and the healer.

Several old philosophical writings on the temple walls salute the Primal--the Source of Being. They are taken from the old Uphanishads, (over two hundred Uphanishads are presently known):

*All Pervasing,*
*The Source of Being,*
*worthy of praise,*
*God in one's abiding worship of Him,*
*the Primal.*

The oldest of the Uphanishads, the Brihadaranyaka (it means the great forest of knowledge), has a strong psychological underpinning with special emphasis and analysis on sleep and dreams. In one of its sections, the state of deep sleep is explored where the reason for lack of sensory experience is taken as the merger of the senses with the perceiver and a doorway to illuminated consciousness. The Vedanta philosophy here opts for a non-dualistic universe in which the nature of reality is Infinite and indescribable, Pure Consciousness and Bliss. This method of negating empirical reality, guiding a disciple from unreality to reality, is a way of observing by constantly reminding oneself: Not this, Not this, or Neti, Neti, a slogan that became famous by latter day Indian masters or gurus such as Ramana Maharishi.

# Devotion at Monkey Temple

Next we went back through the grounds of the BHU where we had passed the library earlier. A building plot is being prepared for new structures. There certainly is action here. Not far from the BHU is the Monkey Temple. Monkeys keep hopping everywhere on temple grounds and inside the temple, monkeys large and small, even tiny newborns and feeding mothers-- yes, mammals like us--behind security gates where no cell phones or cameras are allowed through. Security police are here, not guarding the monkeys so much but on alert for terrorist attacks on the temple and its shrines. Unfortunately there are places where shootings have happened already within the city.

More temple visitors are here in comparison to the New Vishwanath Temple. People are openly devotional, raising their hands, praying even shouting the names of their favorite deities. People of all sorts, ages and classes, buy prasads and sweets to donate and have them blessed by the deities on display be they humanlike figures or animal gods. And, in a side room, one can see an older sadhu talking to a very attentive audience. A well- known teacher-guru, Ramesh says.

We eat some of the blessed sweets on our way back to the same tuk-tuk that had taken us earlier from Old Varanasi to this New City. It's Monday tomorrow and everything will be busy in the streets of Old Varanasi aka Kashi on Shiva's day. One of the statues we saw at the New Vishwanath Temple was a four headed Shiva figure with Shiva, Brahma, Vishnu and Mahesh, each head pointing in one of the four directions. The last mentioned is the Pantheon god that my travel companion from seat 44A mentioned to me on our 257 flight London-Delhi and proclaimed was her God. I need to learn more about Mahesh, the Lord most High; I am encountering His figure here for the first time during my stay.

Now night is falling and sleep soon engulfs me. I feel content to have the white garland put on Shiva's picture in my room and I fall asleep watching it.

What about the praying act and what does prayer do for humans? It takes time to digest what I experienced at the New Vishwanath Temple watching people pray to images and statues and then at the Monkey Temple seeing them bow and pray to an animal god like Hanuman in utter devotion. Perhaps it is the act of praying itself that matters most? However, for a devoted Hindu, images (*murtis*) are not just artistic representations of some theological notion but are God's physical presence. They serve as embodiments. Faith exists in images that are revealed in dreams and believed to contain God's presence. (Visitation dream accounts of Vishnu are for instance well-known in India).

Hanuman will gladden a grieving heart. Have some prasaad, please.

# Goddess All Around

Ramesh intends to give me a necklace with a stone for Shiva power and protection. How about that? Then there is the goddess as Durga being one form of Parvati, the wife of Shiva. Ramesh has a small Durga figure in a shrine in his shop together with a figure of Ganesha. These small figures he covers with fresh flowers every day. A red light bulb at the top of the cupboard where they sit gives the shrine a magic glow. He is devoted to Durga as are so many here in Kashi. He speaks to me about a Mother Goddess temple in the high mountains where he likes to take me next time I visit India. He offers to be my guide and body guard. He goes there reglularly with his mother, a devotee to the goddess at the temple in Katra in Jammu Kashmir, and so is the rest of his family.

After dawn this morning, I sleep again and upon waking, I recall a dream in which I saw a burning house all in flames opposite a friend's house. But when I called people to come with me to help and we opened the door to the lounge, no burning was going on anymore, we only encountered motionless and silent people. Finally in this long dream, the dreamscape changed and I felt I was flying on an airplane over my homefjord Eyjafjordur to land at

Akureyri airport. When overlooking the fjord from the plane, I noticed how brisk and beautiful everything looked and caught Mt. Kaldbakur in panoramic view. A white strong light showed at the top and another equally large in mid mountain. Upon exclaiming: holy mountain, I greet you, I awoke.

Long after and once back home to Iceland when reflecting on that dream, a close family friend becomes critically ill of cancer with no prior warning--it crept upon him silently. But he has survived after having an operation. (A burning house can be taken for a flaming illness in the body according to old Icelandic dream symbolism). Another reflection of the dream has to do with a planned visit to Jammu Kashmir to visit mountains of light, namely, the Trikuta mountains in Katra where one form of goddess Durga named Mata Vaishno Devi is believed to reside in three stone pillars in a cave underground. Whereto Ramesh and his family head every Spring.

Later I meet Biba at Monu, an adopted Italian daughter of Madhav and his wife Indu. She had her newborn son with her--what a beautiful boy--accompanied by her Indian husband. When I looked to greet the infant, I felt he looked like a tiny little man with much black hair. He actually reminded me of someone who had passed at Easter 2011. I had been in Montréal when I received the news. A whole circle of a holy evolution. But what do we know anyhow?

In the afternoon I am in the room writing. After some time the good bird starts chirping, reminding me of Newton our Indian ringneck. Perhaps there is kinship somehow to the chirping from the Birdman at JFK at Easter 2011 on my way N.Y.-Montréal; some bird-telling news? He had greeted me in chirp as he passed me and I spoke back in chirp too! It came naturally to both of us.

Today the two red Hibiscus flowers of the garland given to me by the Brahmin at the New Vishwanath Temple have blossomed and opened while the small white ones making up the garland itself are slowly fading. It is so beautiful to see the red flowers, these favorites of Shiva. Interesting to see if I manage to bring the garland once dry in one piece home.

When young, I loved drying flowers especially the violets that I loved. Later in life, I came to live at Violet Street and have done so for over thirty years where small violets grow among tall trees in our garden at number eight. And, *Sumana* was the first sanskrit name I was given way back in my yoga studies. Sumana for a flower stretching towards infinity.

# Mystery of Doors and Spaces

I recall how father's travels in the UK opened new vistas and served as doors to the broader cosmos of my teenage years. Very often he was over, especially in London and Liverpool for business. Frequently, he took the flight back through Glasgow and that's actually how I made my initial Scotland journey. But to start with, we visited London, Belgravia, parks, exhibitions. There were walks-walks-walks; then we visited Hackney and the factory grounds by the canal.

Later he introduced me to Scotland and Glasgow and the outskirt doors to the Higlands where one could even glimpse some Highland cows grassing in the distance. Decades on, I came to live in the Highlands with my two children of Scottish ancestry in their ancestral glen of Balquhidder where a Buddhist monastery is now located.

Doors are intriguing items in the eyes of children to more and more expansions of their worlds. The door to my Monu room number five is brown with green and blue in middle. Locked with a slam and I unlock with a big key. Doors are symbolic as routes of passage to mystical spaces and other realities. Just like rivers are.

Somehow the space in grandfather's office at my childhood home Brekkugata number three comes to mind with the two big windows from which one could see the tall pine trees and the sacred and beloved sorbus acuparia tree and also the grass lawns farther up, one was called grandpa's lawn where we often played. I loved being in his office, probably that room of my childhood I enjoyed best apart from my own next door. A door had been sealed between the two rooms long before my birth of which I never knew but when I started dreaming repeatedly a door beteen the two rooms that I delighted in walking through and reported those dreams, I was told of the inital design. By then, the dreamer I was around ten to twelve.

Another space I loved was the verandah. A huge beautiful verandah at the back side of the house all in glass except floor and roofing. One could adjust the windows to weather conditions and stay in all year round really. From early childhood onwards, I had many a happy hour rocking in the two rocking chairs, cuddling my doll and teddy and contemplating as I watched the fleeting skies and trees outside. Hoping now to bring my Psychology of Religion and Dreams off the verandah while observing the every day life of my fellow men and women here in rocking Kashi.

Still another space I loved was going through the tiny door to my mum's walk-in-closet and spend many a happy hour there contemplating everything and nothing and sifting through her clothes - a stylish theosophically-minded lady drawing on her French pool of genes - from different periods of fashion. The faint perfume smells, the feel of fabrics and texture still linger. Gifted in language, I just loved sitting and listen to her speak. When they eventually decided to turn the closet into one luxorious bathroom, I was in tears and have only encountered annoying dreams of that transformation!

A containing space such as the walk-in-closet feels secure and nurturing like many of us know who have worked long in psychotherapy. A happy place to be, the womb.

# One White Cow and Her Baby Calf

Again I start my day at Ganga Fuji with my favorite tea of lemon, some banana lassi and plain toast. Same scenery as usual when I walk towards Ganga. An older sadhu in marooni cloth--the same man has been sitting outside Monu for several mornings now--well-built and keeps silent with the Shiva mantra on his forehead. Perhaps *a kavilapa*, a devotee in silent prayer around the clock. He may have been a professor at the uni earlier in his life or maybe he still is, some of the academics mingle like that on their personal pilgrimage in the eternal city.

The cows are out and the police too beside Kali Temple and so we go. Some transcendence in one fleeting moment down by Ganga, experiencing the grand order of things and feeling an intrinsic part with everybody around who are hustling and bustling and begging. A busy mother's way. Will check on Ramesh once back for the trip to Sarnath, he had customers when I passed earlier.

I keep thinking of the sheer gentleness and love showered by a white cow mother on her beautiful white baby calf. I meet them daily here in Kalika gali. What expression of everlasting love and devotion.

# Sarnath in Thunderstorm

All is well here in Varanasi when we leave for Sarnath with the weather rather humid but pleasant. We come to Sarnath after going through Old Varanasi passing the Head Post Office, Malu market, Varuna Bridge, Muslim Territory and eventually entering the boulevards of Sarnath, all nice and clean with towering trees at each side. Sarnath village is very neat and tidy and many houses are freshly painted. We head for the Deer Park, exactly where I want to start.

The sky is strikingly different from Varanasi, you can see it wide and blue with light white mists in panorama. I love it. After buying my ticket of a hundred daal, I stroll towards *Damakha Stupa*, a few heavy raindrops start falling. I walk straight to the stupa feeling the beat of ages passed. How wonderful to stand under a clear blue sky among these majestic trees in the Deer Park and gaze at living history at the place where Buddha gave his first sermon...

Please do not put any more golden foil on His stupa though, I pray--the stupa has been covered with golden foil in some places. Nothing so unauthentic for such a sacred emblem. When I have taken my full tour around the stupa, heavy rain suddenly comes on with thunder washing the fake gold off the stupa and washing me clean too; it gets me totally soaked.

We wait in the car for the rain to stop but in vain so we drive on and pass the Buddha museum and then drive to see the large Buddha statue in light pink at the Temple. Now it is raining cats and dogs and we return to Varanasi. Heavy thunders roll at least four times over our heads as we drive and we can see how the cows, bulls, calves, buffaloes, all love the heavy rainfall, they dance and hop in the rain and mud blissfully happy. Returning to Varanasi, the rainbow is out; a rainbow body is gifted from Heaven.

# A Dewdrop and a Starry Sky

Was this heavy rainfall and raging thunderstorm in Sarnath some cleansing of a hidden stairway to Heaven? Well, it served not only as a blessing to the trees and plants but all the animals rejoiced in it too. What Leela of the Lord those myriad water crystals being bestowed upon us! Then, it brightened up to blue on our way back. Hold this brightness close to the jewel in your heart--*Om mani padme hum*--and stop clowning around when witnessing such a display of celestial splendour. We drive back to Varanasi in awe over a glimpse of enlightenment.

While I write, *Would you know my name if I saw you in Heaven,* now plays at Yogi Lodge from Eric Clapton's *Tears in Heaven* song. In Yogi Lodge there is this beautiful old mantelpiece illustrating a bridal company in Rajasthan. The prince is the predominant figure sitting on a white elephant, a majestic tiger in the background. Amongst the Far Pavillions of Rajasthan some very fine Indian dreamlore on handwritten illustrated manuscripts is preserved.

Dreaming white elephants are nobility dreams. The most famous by far that found its way to all countries of Asia, is the white elephant dream of Buddha's mother Maya signalling His conception so often presented in literature and illustrated in religious art. Maya saw the following dream: the four guardians of the world lifted her on her couch and carried her to the Himalayan mountains and placed her under a great sala tree. Then their queens bathed her and dressed in heavenly garments, anointed Maya with perfumes and put garlands of heavenly flowers on her, replaid her on the heavenly coach with her head towards the east. Now, the future Buddha wandering as a superb white elephant approaches her from the north. Holding a white lotus in his trunk, he circumbulates her three times. Then he gently strikes her right side and enteres her womb.

In Buddhist dreamlore, one can find the following remarks:

*So in dreams we cross*
*the limits of the world*
*and reach the Infinite.*

They say there are several heavens over that eternal mount Meru (be it where it may be), one of those proclaimed thirty three is the *Tushita* heaven, the special field of Gautama Buddha, Lord Maitreya to come. Kalachakra or the Wheel of Time is turning the tide and a new cosmological chess game is on. Animal Tamer's vision of the alive Buddha statue in the living room before leaving for Kashi feels just as natural within a given cosmological context, and so also is the experience of a deity residing at the centre of a mandala or at the innermost triangle of a yantra or the worship of an animal deity. A question of how we look when the universe glimpses at us. In a dewdrop and a starry sky, there are multiple fields and heavens. Some beautiful mathematics.

Today is Gandhi's day October 2 and also Siggi's birthday--the British-American-Icelandic born father of my two children--who made his final transfer at the Spring Equinox in 2009.

# The Void and Crystal Awareness

How simple and down to earth this visit to Buddha's Sarnath had been. Life is simple and good, so watch out! Both life and death are the birthrights of every human being and to be celebrated; every individual dies only once in his or her lifetime; the dignity of the dying should be preserved.

There is a growing tendency in our modern world not to face the fact of death and to avoid feelings of being nothing and to fear a state of not existing. Instead, the inclination to gain pleasure and fill us up with material gains is on the increase. Underneath, an alienation not only from death but from life itself, creeps in. In the midst of everyday settings and consuming, we tend to loose ourselves and forget we are alive and must die.

Practicing *mindfulness* is a way of waking up and become more aware of the dreamlike nature of waking consciousness and also to grow in dream awareness. We must at the same time learn to ground us when going about our daily duties. Constant watchfulness would help centre us beyond the personal.

The progressive thinker and architecht Buckminster Fuller was in for the greatest surprise of his lifetime when at his wife's deathbed she halfconscious still managed to reach for his hand. At that, Fuller gave up his own breath and passed while holding her hand. A mutual transfer in utter compassion after a lifetime of dedicated work within the philosophy of form, structure, and evolution. In his cosmological outlook on things, he thought of us earthlings as a process or function when he said: *I seem to be a verb, an evolutionary process, an integral function of the universe.*

Here in Kashi, ineffable and energetic experiences in light are encountered in my night-time and daytime visions. I have no words for them; am I experiencing the Void? Crystal awareness? I recall what I learnt in the eighties about the mysteries of language learning and conceptual development at Stirling when working on my doctoral thesis that there are issues that we do not yet have words for. They are at such a deep and sublime level of non-reperesentational imagery, some mathematical realities being examples.

In the spiritual teachings of India into illumination, the growth of consciousness is seen as passing through much sensational mindstuff in evolving mindfulness to the heightening of waking and dreaming experiences - *lucid dreaming* being one such state - that take us from darkness to the Inner Light, to the Void. A door to the Inifinite, the Supreme, Moksha, Nirvana, Liberation. In the Taittiriya Uphanishad the borderland of sleep and dreams is spoken of, the dreamer when *wandering in this borderland, he beholds behind him the sorrows of this world and in front of him, he sees the joys of the beyond.*

Lucid dreaming is a well known phenemenon in Iceland. In our 2003 Skuggsja-Gallup study over half the population had themselves experienced being lucid in their dreams, being aware they were dreaming. Consciousness being conscious of itself. Thus, the lucid dream state renders fine examination of the multiplicity and multidimensionality of dreaming consciousness. And we find that lucid dreaming as a part of spiritual practice is deeply rooted such as the intermediate state of dreams within Tibetan Buddhism for instance that includes daytime and night-time yoga practice as an integral part of spiritual practice.

Still another is the practice of the *Phowa*-preparation for death, a part of the teachings on Dzogchen into Great Perfection. Practicing lucid dreaming as preparation for dying is an age-old method in which incubation and lucid dreaming are used to illuminate the mind and prepare the person for upcoming death. Controlling the dream is practiced for generating a subtle dreambody to eventually accomplish the *clear light of dreams* and to recognize the *clear light of death*.

When it comes to sustaining dream awareness, learning self-reflectiveness prescribed by contemplation practices is needed as well. Meaning we need to learn to be mindful and compassionate in our wake and dream.

# Playin' and being Play'd

Now to some photographs I had promised Animal Tamer. I hope they work out well from the rooftop. The swallows are out and so are the boys with kites. The swallows seem to be playing with them and enjoying the game as they drift easily up and down around the colorful kites.

The sky has cleared just before sunset and from Monu's rooftop I now see two newborn monkey babies. They are so very tiny and fragile looking but already hopping about however weakly. And I can see the white cow beneath with her calf come walking along the gali. She heads for that cool place in the gali next to Kali temple. She just walks on her own with the calf confidently knowing her way like the humans. There is a spin of stars across the night sky and I head down for my room to hear Amitir play from Yogi Lodge the gentle music of *Daddy, daddy cool...* As the moon arces across the sky I fall into benign sleep.

The bird sang long and well at dawn. Nothing else was heard for quite some time, then few voices, footsteps, things being moved about. The dog was quiet at the onset of this wonderful day. Yeah; we are into mid October and it's cooler--the first morning it feels like that and I do not wake up in sweath! Nights are getting colder and we soon are in for winterlike weather that will go on for some months.

Time has passed quickly in this retreat of mine with half-fasting, meditating, praying, dreaming, writing, reading and saying praise. I feel good about it all and hopeful for my next steps. *Shahib* is an honorary title for someone like a doctor. And for the first time in my life, I was called shahib this morning. It was Madhav smiling in his mischievous manner so characteristic of him. In the night when I woke from my dreams, I had this wonderful sight of walking on the university grounds near the Psychology Department and feeling much focussed energy surrounding everything.

There is a lot going on in this vibrant hurly-burly medieval city of God. One is the custom of emotional business--playing on people's emotions--selling them God. Making them feel special, that they are performing good deeds and enhanching their karmas by giving funds when only some of the money will be used for real cause. An old and new way of hoarding gold aka modern cash by exploitation.

Yeah; the cash flow goes mostly in the direction of greed like elsewhere. When I ask my friends about this custom, they say God is everywhere and Ramesh adds that *Shiva is not affected by such worldy means, He is eternal and above it all.* But they are not happy about the trend and feel of what is going on with this kind of selling and exploiting. The final transfer is sacred and so is Kashi and they have seen their family and friends being cremated at the holy Ganga not to be taken lightly. It follows that not everybody has the funds for cremation on Ganga banks.

Oxford professor and a devoted researcher of Icelandic dreamlore Gabriel Turville-Petre claimed that we go back to our dreams and dreaming when value systems and social intstitutions fail us--go back to the roots for answers. Dreaming a new world into being: Hindus believe that through Vishnu's dreaming, a sea-change in consciousness takes place and the universe is born anew.

Indifference is one form of violence in the modern world and an indifferent attitude is prevailing in much human encounter. Therefore, we do not take necessary action; what a destructive fashion of the times we live in. No wonder the world is so broken and people so damaged. People tend to take this indifferent attitude for a calm, objective mind. Plain nonsense they have sold themselves. Far from it. We must cherish dreaming once more in order to re-connect with compassion and mercy and proceed forth.

# Durga is Here

I am in tears over the growing drug problem after seeing today two young people doped and haltering in the gali. The same smart laws abide in the drug trade here as elsewhere in the world, harsh with sneaky manipulations all along. Young people breaking away from the conditional societal bonds and taking to drugs. Buying the lie of their dealers and the drug culture that they are freeing themselves from the traps of conventional culture, instead getting enslaved in an ever more hostile subculture where nobody cares once funds are gone. Enslaved in a lifelong prison if they are not smart enough to get out in time. Yeah; I've seen them here, dopers and junkers. Young Westerens with diminishing lights in their eyes and matted auras in a poppy heaven or a hellish bootcamp depending.

On my stroll this morning down the Kalika gali, my neighbour dog was running down also. He was on his own, very confident and had a painted white Shiva dot on his forehead. Then there was a black big Nandi bull near Kali Temple with a garland of orange flowers and another garland of read and white ones around his broad neck. I wonder what's up today? All the animals here keep their special characters such as the barking dog next door. And that big black bull. Then the sadhu who sits out front is giving a sermon. A crowd of people sits by his feet listening attentively. The weather is good and many people and cows are out and about near the entrance to Dashaswamedhghat. No sadhus are sitting in a row here like the other day however. In their place we now have tons of bikes and motorbikes. It looks like a forest, a huge gear forest.

A boat guide comes asking me questions on my visit. Many devotees are streaming into the city because of the upcoming Durga festival starting on the fourteenth, he explains. I've given my respect to Durga all the times I've passed Her shrine in the gali. Her shrine looks all cleaned up today and someone is arranging flowers. He is ordinarily dressed, perhaps the flower man? Some women with babies are begging, very few give anything at all, give my usual thirty to fourty daals. Saddens me in many ways to see this trade, I must say. But such is life on the street in Varanasi in this day and age with Durga blessing all affairs of humans and fighting evil amongst them at the same time. In the ancient forest books, we find:

*Is there any state of
existence which may be
free from suffering,
ignorance and grief,
and be full of unbound joy.*

*Just as a bird looses its*
*freedom*
*when it is endorsed so*
*those are ever doomed*
*to bondage*
*who are enslaved*
*to desires.*

# Holy Cow and Holy Shit

Another day has broken and upon waking, a thought of the white cow and her baby calf is on my mind. I keep wondering if I came here to be initiated by a cow, a holy cow, into a blissful stream of her loving kindness? Being daily fed with her milk and lassi.

I never heard the dog howl nor the bird chirp for so long as at dawn this morning. Now I have learnt that the brown-red dog lives next door indeed and I have caught a glimpse of his owner when taking out his bike to ride down the gali with doggie proudly following master. Still struggling with the dog's name though. The dog sat for quite some time at my feet after breakfast at Yogi's when chatting to Ramesh. I've learnt that he lives with his owner upstairs the weaver's shop. Actually adjacent to the same floor as my Monu room is. No wonder I hear him so clearly day and night through the walls.

Last night, I had some mystic dreams of flowing animals. These dreams took place in Iceland, some were related to my job once working with schools in the countryside, the scenery reminded of our grandparents village. Other dreams happened at my family home and were staged in the kitchen and in our Stulla's playroom. For instance, in here was a tiny turtle flowing that could grow from being tiny into a large one--she loved staying in a beautiful bowl near the stairs. In went also a flowing bear, one white, one brown-black, and a flowing snake! They all went (flew) to the same place as the turtle, they went there because they, like her, loved being here and at the same time were harmless at that special spot.

Raining cats and dogs in Varanasi today after our visit to Sarnath yesterday. The rain came on suddenly at the Ganga after doing my usual puja at noon down at Dashaswamedh. I am writing down the story of the ghat; the mythology of the Horsegate runs that when Ordainer and Grandsire Brahma visited the Holy River on horse (swamedh), He performed ten (das) sacrifices for the benefit of all beings. Also known as the Doorstep of Brahma – *Brahma Dunar* - and is the mot popular ghat in Varanasi and the hub of pilgrims; here the fire ceremony as accords with the ancient customs takes place every night. When dotting down the main story from the stone column at the ghat's entrance, a long slim red-brown animal runs by my feet--quite finehaired like newly combed--and I wondered if she sensed the rain coming on and was taking shelter so she wouldn't be drowned by the rising levels of the river in the heavy rain now pouring down?

But the rain stops equally suddenly as it fell. Feels good to be outside but humid. As I pass, I notice that the upper floors of the buildings on the Vishwanath gali are truly occupied, I had often wondered if anyone really lived there--some are having ironrails before windows while others have laundry hanged in the windows. And house prizes are getting up.

Some strange but somewhat sweet smell is in the air. Are they burning cowshit or dung today for *vibuthi* that claylike ash they put on pilgrims foreheads as Shiva dots in the Golden Temple? Where we now have rows of pilgrims piling up for entry not minding the watery and muddy galis where they wait. Or getting dirty; they know Shiva will cleanse them pure.

# Web of Life and Vibe of Scifi

Today at the ghat I saw two very big and beautiful butterflies. They were of black and orange color and when spreading their wings, the sunlit sky shone through. How perfect. After a whole week in Varanasi, I feel I've sunk into the web of life and I am now noticing the living whereabouts and habitats better. Everything is under guard around the clock because of the nearby sacred shrines and temples. An entrance to one of the four entrances of the Golden Temple is closeby. It is named the *Gate of Luck*. And, near the crossroads of the galis, we have The Golden Temple, the Kali temple, and the Nepalese temple, a Durga shrine and a Ganesha shrine.

Daily, I meet Westerners in the main streets and side-galis of all ages and cultures even with their young infants. A young Indian boy--clean and well-dressed--like most children I meet here, is eating chips from a bag and his younger brother stands in the doorway to their home. Many locals live upstairs of the shops, restaurants, guesthouses, and farms. Yeah; farms are amidst it all, sheds at the back, and I've been visiting a few already. The cows are well looked after by their proud owners and caretakers, some of whom are young boys playing with kites from the rooftops in their spare time in the late afternoon.

The vibe is scifi amongst those worn out habitats; the gear and gadgets of modern technology are all over the place and the sadhus are out too. Not only bikes and motorcycles but other machinery - just as well to be good at driving here in this crazy traffic - cell phones are everywhere and computer facilites around the corner. Modes of transfer abound. Perhaps I'll ring father in the great Hereafter? But no. Even with the omnipotent feel of modern technology, there are limits... The final transfer of a lived lifetime is sacred and there are no easy means of crossing.

Nevertheless, dreaming is a gift to explore limits, a timeless mode of crossing and encountering (with or without technology) as according to ancient belief, dreaming takes place at the threshold between life and death. Dreaming and dying as a natural process in the final transfer is a familiar topic in Indian myth, and other classical texts, and through my research, I've found that fortunately this topic is resurfacing in modern research and literature in India.

# The Gift of Dreaming

These early October nights are still warm but I am adjusting. Means I am waking up several times during sleep and noting down my dreamlife. I don't understand though how people here endure good sleep without modern airconditioning. Even with one in the room, I keep sweathing in pink.

Whatever the culture or the period, people have always questioned themselves about the nature and significance of their dreams and their daily occupations. Some time ago, I came upon this book on sleep and dreams in Indian tradition based on papers--many in sanskrit--given at an international conference at Paris Sorbonne in 2004. A remarkable book on the Indian dream heritage. It reminds me of my ancestor Reverend Saemundur *the learned* at Oddi in South Iceland and his dreams--he had studied at Sorbonne. A gifted dreamer who had prophetic skills and could see the future in his dreams and visions. A gift still running in the family that we now honor with our Icelandic Institute for Dream Studies--Skuggsja--in North Iceland in my hometown of Akureyri.

A beautiful soft night it has been after all the rainfall and the best sleep and rest I've had for long. At one time into morning, I woke up from a *Big dream*: an aura of gentleness surrounded the room and embraced me. As my consciousness was bathed in a soft white light, it opened to wider fields and everything fell in place. I came to realize that there sure exist other fields just as real as the ones we take for granted everyday.

Babaji's voice I heard, humourosly calling out: *Such romantic, you've always been.* Referring perhaps to my father whom I now noticed standing in the room, nodding and smiling. He came by my bedside then moved around on both legs fully dressed up in white, looking smart like a raj. Silently talking to me. The very first dream I have had of him after his death at Easter 2012 with normal walk and talk. What grace. He had been without walk and talk the last years of life.

# *Seeing* a Dream for Direction

Whatever dreams may be, they are meaningful to us earthlings and often offer much console and rekindle hope such as after the death of a loved one. *Seeing a dream* is the Indian expression whereas we in the West say *having a dream*. During the early phases of sleep, Hindu dreamlore claims that some dreams that we see carry certain indications or messages that direct us in our lives. In Iceland, the dreams towards morning when the dreamer is rested should be especially tended.

When I speak to people here about dreams, they associate them with the guidance God can give one through dreaming like Kailash explained this morning at Ganga Fuji over breakfast. The locals also comment on the prophetic nature of dreams. Both these speculations are similar to what one might get when asking modern Icelanders about their belief in dreams. According to our Skuggsja-Gallup survey of 2003, over 70% of the Icelandic population belief dreams are meaningful, give guidance and warning and can be precognitive.

Dreams have been part of popular tradition throughout the ages and as such, have acted as omens in Indian culture, prophetic dreams being commonly present in religious biographies. For instance, Buddhists justified various events in the Buddha's life with the existence of prophetic dreams which seem to relate the historical and the real biography to its spiritual nature. These dreams punctuate not only the mental life of the Buddha but also characters closely related to him, his mother being not the only one since his father was also visited by precognitive dreams.

Besides, the prophetic nature of dreams is clearly evidenced by some of the old Hindu manuscripts and dreams also figure promininently in old initiatory rituals. Certainly, the belief of seeing the future in dreams remained for ages a major element in every day life in India as it did in Iceland and still does.

# One Long Dream or *Deergha Svapna*

Heading now for the Baba Black Sheep circuit to hunt for dream books; I am entering a reflective reading mode. To the left, I find a good bookshop at Godowlia, *The City Bookshop*, and learn that the Hindu woman owner has strong links with Scotland and regularly visits her sister who lives in Dundee. She has one book on dreams but has not yet got the book on death and dying and dreams that I am hunting, *A Dream for the Dying* published recently based on dream reports from Tamil Nadu. I too keep visiting Scotland and Stirling where I did my Ph.d. studies in Psycholinguistics and Developmental Psychology. Long before that we had our Scottish links through visits with our father. Besides, my parents-in-law always kept their connections with their relatives--the Magnussons in Edinburgh.

On coming out, I notice quite a few large white and grey horses being showered clean and then neatly brushed by their drivers with their carriages at a closeby open stadium. This mode of driving in Varanasi is still an ongoing business.

I learn from *Universal Book* (the bookstore at the other side of Godowlia) with their good selection of dreambooks that dreams reflect a hidden part of ourselves and the universe and that Indian philosophers defined the nature of the real world as being a long dream from which one awakes from once its nature is known. Hence, the old philosophers analyzed the position of dreams in their study of the states of consciousness. Modern researchers have pointed out that dreams cross over intellectual boundaries, that they sweep into any and every aspect of artistic and literary material once one looks closely. They argue that the abundance of this material reveals how dreams have held and still hold a major position in Indian religion, law and monastic rules, how they interfered in the daily life of the dreamer and how they were perceived and paved way to higher spiritual or psychological levels.

Already in the ancient forest books--some of which were composed in Kashi--such as the Uphanishads there are many reflections on dreams and dreaming. The Upanishads distinguish four states of consciousness: waking, dreaming, dreamless sleep, and a transcendant absolute fourth state of *turiya* in which the individual is identical with the Universal Spirit, the well-known Atman-Brahman identity. The four states are not discrete but blend into each other. The waking state is seen as a distorted image of the fourth state while the dreaming and dreamless states are the intermediate steps to turiya. From the viewpoint of the absolute, turiya is more real than the other states; waking is then but a long dream, named *deergha svapna*.

In academic circles today there is speculation that dreaming is a continuous process that takes place in waking life as in sleep. Like an unbroken riverflow. In the West, we have hitherto spoken of a distinction between waking and dreaming and timed it after our cycadic clock whereas the

Hindu and Buddhist traditions talk of different states of consciousness in dreams, that we continuously dream.

One of the Western founders of modern dream theory and research Carl Gustav Jung speculated on the issue and came to the conclusion that we probably dream all the time; while our waking consciousness makes so much noise, we do not hear the dream. And recent publications on the history of sleep in the West have shed light on the fact that before the onset of street-gaslightings and the Industrial Revolution in the 18th and 19th century, people in Europe generally slept for two four hour periods over night, then awoke for one or two hours in between and contemplated their dreams.

Recalling now father's early morning wakes - Hindus name it *Brahma Muhurt* - and his mode of being able to naturally go into a deep contemplative mode or easily fall into a light or deep sleep on and off during the day. Sleep, wake, dream for twenty four hours. It helped him much in his severe condition and through many a difficult operation. And, when prepared to pass, he made a gentle, light transfer fully conscious, out of all sedatives and other medication.

# Dream Whispers

Dreams whisper to us daily; often a vague whisper is all we hear, and we keep forgetting them. Other dreams whisper differently, and we intuitively feel we must tend them.

Whether dreams and dreaming are presently gaining enough attention in practices is an open question in modern India. But then again, one could find everything in terms of religion and dreams, I suppose, be it deep or superficial, in this multi-layered city of Kashi Vishwanath. Is it for instance common practice to read dreams, narrate them and analyze over the breakfast table? And, is there use of dreams in daily practice in ashrams in order to reach higher states of consciousness? Dreams may indeed be underestimated in importance in present-day India, not topping the charts of superfluous living as scholars have warned. Then, you can't help but notice them wherever you go as images of dreams and sleep in art are present in this eternal city of Dream.

The acts of sleeping and dreaming being a source of life are seen in various aspects of old Buddhist, Jain and Brahmanical art. Representations of Vishnu's Cosmic Sleep in sculpture figure prominently, especially in Nepalese tradition. One dream of the young future Buddha related Him to Vishnu sunk in His cosmic sleep. As dreams are had while sleeping and dreaming, gods lie down and from the depth of their sleep, life is thought to arise. They dream the world into existence. Illustrated in artistic iconographies of Vishnu reclining on the snake Ananata--symbolic of the Inifinite, of Eternity--dreaming the universe into being. Perhaps Vishnu sleeps in the Nepalese temple down by sacred Ganga? I must pay a visit. Further, the goddess in her various froms such as Tara has had many expressions in both illustrated manuscripts and sculptures on dreams and omens over the ages.

A core concept of Hindu ideaology is that physiologically and psychologically we are a part of a broader cosmology and slumber and dream most of the time. Thus, our world is but the dream of our created world of *Maya*, a fleeting illusion. Comparative research in all the ancient traditions speak of the path of dreaming as a way to gain deeper insights thru spiritual dreams and eventually gain enlightenment. Dreams and other states of consciousness such as mystical experience can open the heart and mind for transformation to take place and a higher cosmic consciousness to be experienced. Not surprisingly, such transfer is described in many of the old sanskrit prescriptive texts. The role of dreams in other religions than Hindu and Buddhist has had much influence in India as well. Similar emphases and practices are found in Jainism, the mysticism of Christian and Jewish traditons, and Muslim.

Dream yoga is one branch of yoga initially practiced in Tibet and the High Himalayas having been introduced over past decades to Indian mainstream and over recent decades to the West. Dreams and dream figures are here seen as *real* as anything can be. The role of dreams in accessing higher waters of consciousness used to be practiced in the Hindu ashrams. There is the Ayurvedic perception of dreams in hand with the Hindu experience of dreaming and respect for the meaning of dreams. Even the therapeutic value of dreams is spoken of by Charaka in Ayurveda and how dreams can facilitate diagnoses and treatment. This founder of Ayurvedic medicine lived around 300 BC or aeons before the birth of Western Psychology and its founding fathers, Sigmund Freud, Carl Gustav Jung and William James. Dreams are likewise considered in a medical context, being at the threshold between life and death and formulating a message from the unseen world which can be analyzed and lend to the application of remedies. Health clinics in Varanasi are many dedicated to Ayurveda and several yoga centres and ashrams are devoted to some special gurus. Hopefully dream practices in Kashi are regaining ground.

# Dreamin' Psychology at Uni

Today I am going with Ramesh for a visit to the Psychology Department at Banares Hindu University or BHU that is now celebrating its 50th anniversary. And happen to meet someone who knows the university and its departments quite well and offers to take us on a tour. Once we reach the BHU grounds, Ramesh tells me that his cousin is going to meet us here at the entrance to the New Vishwanath Temple and take us around. To my great surprise, the cousin student turns out to be the young man from next door Monu with the motor bike and owner of my dog friend, (quite a dreamer that dog and needless to mention, keeps whining in sleep). Now studying law, but already holds a degree in horticulture and botany. Of an old Brahmin caste, one Prashant Mishra.

Prashant introduces me to the Head of the Psychology Department, Professor Indramani Singh, who then calls a meeting with some of the other Professors at which we discuss dreams in Iceland and India. Plans for a crosscultural dream research are on the drawing board. The elderly professor to my right has strong links with my old university at Stirling and the Dementia Services Development Centre (DSDC) over there. I had given a talk on sleep and dreams among the elderly at their York conference in 2009. The BHU and

DSDC have done some mutual research and exchanges recently. A small world and a good one for the matter. Full of synchronicities. A wonderful visit and quite a successful dreamin' session.

Speaking of good company, from Swethasvatara Upanishad, one reads:

*There are four methods*
*of crossing over*
*the ocean of worldly existence*
*namely*
*tranquility, contentment*
*company of the good or the wise,*
*and thinking.*

# Vehicles of Transformation

Generally speaking, dreams are tools allowing a reading of the mind, life and world. They hold a function in literary discourse, be it classical or contemporary similar to our Icelandic dream heritage as is found for example in many of our Icelandic sagas, and often are sources of much inspiration. They can also be prophetic in Indian religious biographies or in the popular tradition, the same holds true for my homeland. Discriminating which dreams are prophetic and of significance is a way of learning to move in the world of dreams and whether they are dreamed under sepcial conditions and or special phases during night.

Then it is the question of reading or interpreting dreams and their symbols. Dream symbolism abounds in the spritiual and religious traditions and is found when exploring how dreams are represented in practice, language and literature. Western perspectives are present here in modern India where one can find the western view on dreams based on modern psychology and sleep research into *NONREM* and *REM* sleep--stages of restful sleep and dream-sleep. Comparative studies of dreams obviosuly suggest the existence of a system of dream interpretation.

Interest in dreams ran central in Buddhism but did not remain limited to Buddha's life. For instance, Tibetan monks also practiced the art of dreaming and perceived dreams as a powerful source of inspiration. The presence of the five dreams of the Bodhisvatta in the *Murals of Pagan* is an example.

Last night, I kept seeing a special mask of an animal face in my dreams. It was of grey, blue and green colours and I wondered what it could mean? Perhaps a mask reflecting one of those Hindu deities, a rat or a mouse most likely. Wondered if masked deities were common dream themes as there is an old tradition behind the Indian puppet and masks. Thoughts of Jung come to mind and his ideas of dolls and puppets and masks and the *collective unconscious.*

During sleep our awareness reaches the land of dreams and we not only *see* or *have* a dream but also we *feel* much as dreams have many emotional aspects. Some dreams as stated by Jung and others, are of a strong arcehetypal imagery, rooted in mankind's mutual heritage of its ancient past, our *collective unconscious.* The *Hero* and the *Villain* being examples of such archetypes often reflected in myths and epics.

Dreams are described in all aspects of Indian literature where they hold a function in the literary discourse similar to our Icelandic sagas in which dreams often predict the saga's main events and tell of the destinies of key characters or heroes and heroines. Occuring in classical narrative, dramatic or epic texts or in contemporary Tamil short stories, dreams abound.

Dreams play an overhelmingly dominant role in religious and philosophical literature in the epics, Vedas, Puranas and Shastras, as reports of sleep and dreams in the famous epics of *Ramayana* and Mahabharata witness. In Ramayana, the Hindus most popular epic, there are records of many precognitive dreams. One expample being when King Dashrath dies, his sons have forewarning dreams of his upcoming death. Another dream is the one of Hanuman and Sita when they dream of setting Lanka on fire, eventually the hero Lord Rama breaks all barriers and conquers his opponents over beloved Sita. In the Mahabharata another heroic tale there are several accounts of dreams such as the famous dream of Gandhari of a tree bearing ripe berries, she then becomes a mother to one hundred sons, the Kuravas, the opposing clan to the righteous Pandavas. Around the battle of those two clans the epic is woven.

Vocabulary used to refer to dreams and sleep in Indo-European languages proves to have been extremely diversified and rich as the Oxford professor Turville-Petre pointed out in his research into the Icelandic dream heritage. He had studied under Hobbit and Lord of the Rings author J.R. Tolkien and through him became fascinated with Nordic mythology and Icelandic dreamlore eventually to visit Iceland frequently. Old narrative material shows that not all dreaming is nice and tender--some dreams are threathening and we even find techniques against bad dreams. Strong belief has always existed in dreams as channels of intercourse with supernatural powers and in channelled messages from other realms hence visitation dreams are common of passed loved ones and this holds true for both Iceland and India.

While in Kashi, I have come upon this dream-prayer in my reading: *May we be lost in the dream beyond life and death alike.*

# Flame and Smoke at Manikarnika

Now the day has come to enter Manikarnika, go visit the Burningghat. But not from the main street gali like I first thought I would but from Meerghat, a small steep ghat that takes you straight to the river. As the river floor is particularly low today, one can easily walk ghat to ghat on shore. So, I started at noon after puja at Dasaswamedh and one Prateep accompanied me. He proved a wonderful guide on this riverbank route.

Prateep told me about the guesthouses as we passed like the popular Alka guesthouse that so many Westerners visit, and the Widow's guesthouse, a tall old marooni building with balconies overlooking the Ganga for Hindu widows. Some coming to pray for the safe transfer of their deceased husbands and their hopes for a blissful dwelling in the great Hereafter or to prepare their own crossing. And already at Meerghat there are free houses where people from remoter parts of India can come to for lodging while pilgrimaging. Many pilgrims come from South India.

Coming from their bath at Ganga, a middle aged Hindu dressed in orange and his companion a Western woman in an orange sari greet us with their Shiva mantras painted on their foreheads. People and animals bathe all along the route and the boats are out. We catch sight of some sheep bathing in the river. And some goats and buffalos splashing in it too. Animals have tramped the banks so it's pretty muddy and slippery all the way to Manikarnika.

A tiny fragile looking old sadhu sits under the balcony to the Nepalese Temple's adjoining buildings to our destined ghat. He has a picture of Shiva and his consort Parvati in front of him which he seems to meditate upon. What a peaceful aura as we pass. We now have clear sights of the Burningghat with people in piles on the side balconies, bodies are being burnt, and one can see the flames and smoke rise higher. *Shiva is here*, Prateeb says, *if one cannot find Him anywhere else*. A solemn nod; I am lost to flames and smoke in contemplation.

On our way back, we come across that old sadhu again, soon to gasp his last breath, I remark. Prateeb explains there are hospices for old people like him down by Manikarnika where they can come to upon dying. May the old man be blessed and so his transfer.

# Lord of Animals at Nepalese Temple

Dedicated to Lord Pushupati or Pashupati - the Lord of animlas - we are now at the steep doorsteps to the Nepalese Temple at Lakshighat--the ghat bears the name of a Nepalese princess. It has the same layout and style but is of course much smaller than the famous Pushupati Temple in Nepal, Shiva's Temple. Here was a wonderful quiet place to come to for river and meditation some twenty years ago Prateep explains but that has changed with all the tourists.

A young man from the mother temple in Nepal is collecting entry fees at a small counter by the platform. Upon paying and entering we see beautiful carvings in stone from the Kama Sutra on the sidewalls some being one to two hundred years old. At the temple itself in mid space we see delicately cut out wooden carvings of the Hindu deities.

The temple is locked off, it's high noon and someone is sleeping inside, perhaps going for a cosmic nap? Instead we take to the lovely view from the balcony towards Ganga beneath a sloping old tree and greet a large statue of Nandi in garland, the largest I've come across so far in Kashi. Shiva being the Lord of animals and the bull Nandi, His mode of travel thru the earthly and heavenly realms. You have been a trusted fellow for long Nandiji and carried me through and through. For instance, your name surfaced in my final psycholinguistic experiment for the doctorate, the bright-eyed pixie - a forest and flower caretaker - bore your name in a story on how children come to learn new words and grow vocabulary from within a given context. The language (including text) that we hear is not only of a cognitive character--it is also audial, even musical, symbolic and of an implicate order; holographic.

# A Fleeting Dream of *Me* and the Supreme Reality of *That*

What are people after in Kashi anyway; our minds never being fully satisfied? Why do they bother sit and stare at nothing and everything those yogis or sadhus and sannyasis? Well, the lesson in this oldest of cities seems that we must indeed *die* to *live* and *be real*. Being real is a fringe question of reality. Highly trained yogis and mystics are said to not only visit Supreme reality but reside there most of the time. They rather experience our world as a fleeting dream.

Rumi, the great sufi poet, spoke of *mystic death* on one's way to the Supreme, and so did Saint Theresa of Avila whom I had written of in my BA thesis within the field of the Psychology of Religion on mystical and religious experiences and their transformative quality on personality. St. Theresa proclaimed that she had to empty her mind of everything, leave behind all conceptions of herself and identify with nothing on her path towards sacredness. Henceforth, you must *die before thou diest*.

The asleep-awake boundary interests modern dream researchers during which dreamers report experiencing the flux of shifting realities. And throughout night, we keep shifting between dreamless sleep and dream sleep. At the vague boundaries between waking and falling asleep - the so called *hypnagogic* state - the mind sometimes feels blown out of its conventional comfort, dreamers report seeing all sorts of shapes and colors and might even hallucinate. From a developmental standpoint, the idea that the I or ego is not the only reality and that here are layers and layers of consciousness is something that we must embrace in order to move forward.

Deep sleep - awakeness is another situation that many long-time meditators speak of. In the sleep state, the dream maybe going on but the dreamer is aware of a calm, uninvolved luminous sense of awareness that observes the dream but is in no way identified with any part of it. Some mindfulness in a sleeping mode. The Uphanishads speak of *That thou art*, maintaining that what remains when everything else, every identification, is dropped, cannot be *me* but an impersonal *That*. In such deep sleep no sense of I exists as yogi master Ramana Maharishi once described, only *Pure Consciousness*. Says his Bombay born disciple Nisargadatta Maharaj:

*In reality there is only one state;*
*when distorted by self-identification*
*it is called a person,*
*when coloured with the sense of being*
*it is the witness;*
*when colourless and limitless,*
*it is called the Supreme.*

The East-West views on the relationship between the dreaming and waking states differ. Historically in the West, the two are seen as discontinuous phenomena although empirical ecvidence from contemporary dream research has begun to challenge the notion of impermeable boundaries between dreaming and waking. As mentioned earlier, the boundaries are more permeable in Hindu, specifically the Uphanishadic thought which has influenced traditonal views in India on the relationship between the dreaming and waking states.

# Kashi Vishwanath at the Golden Temple

Well, now is the day to go visit the Kashi Vishwanath--the Golden Temple of Lord Shiva. Hopefully I'll get in. No money to bring with you as they don't want people to bring in a lot of cash while visiting. I feel an inkling of excitement in my stomach over finally going into the Golden Temple. Let's see if the time is right around five this afternoon, it should have settled down by then, the long row of pilgrims waiting for hours to enter.

No queue, I just walk straight in. What a surprise this long awaited visit is! All went well with getting through the Gate of Luck with Ramesh helping. He waited outside in a friend's shop from whom I bought a flower basket for offerings. I head straight for the Holy Cow goddess Anapurna Temple. Looks pretty, quite large, much of it in red. I feel totally at peace, a calm mind, not coming here to ask for anything only to pay respects. But alas, after giving an offering of a violet flower to goddess Anapurna, I meet a young sadhu sitting there to one side pushing for money. He gave me a dark orange band of good fortune that he insisted on wrapping around my wrist. An old man was sitting beside him. I gave them one dollar and ten daals and got away. What a surprise this emotional business inside the holy abode of the great cow goddess, the sustainer of life. But the atmosphere felt lovely inside Her temple and a strong flow of high energy as I uttered prayers to the large statue at the centre.

Next I wanted to go to the Golden Temple and had to show my passport and other information to the police, they wrote down where I live while here. Then I was eventually allowed to enter the sacred Temple of Vishwanath and once here, I could see the whole layout of the Temple grounds and the smaller shrines. So this is the Golden Temple, it feels homely, not stately, to my great relief.

Once inside, I was adviced by a gentle police officer to go straight to the jyotir shrine that stands in the middle of the whole platform. In there I gave a flower garland from my basket to an old Brahmin who was uttering some mantras into the running waters over a large black lingam, naked except for his tiny breechcloth, very agile for his age though. Somehow the thought of a cobra came to mind. He put the garland around the lingam and looked me straight in the eye, and I looked at the jyotir. At that moment I was engulfed in a cosmic vision where I felt the aeons come swirling from the watered lingam and I was taken through times past, present and future, and could watch universes and galaxies swirling whilst I prayed for the good of all beings.

Then all of a sudden after blessing me, the Brahmin swung a huge garland over me that he had just wet in the running water. This garland was of white, orange and marooni flowers with silver threads woven in between them and green leaves (this I observed better once back at Monu). I got wet from water dripping on my head and shoulders and wondered if the garland was bigger than me and if I could carry it without falling down? I stumbled back in astonishment and felt I saw a faint smile on the Brahmin's face. I smiled at him gratefully, feeling quite taken aback by this powerful experience and thinking the Vishwanath jyotir certainly is of a great universal force.

I felt numb when outside and noticing that the shrine I had just visited had indeed been the Golden Temple itself, as I now noticed the guilded spire and the black Shiva flag at the top. Perhaps there had been a silent unconscious question on my mind before entering on the manifoldness of time and time cycles? I had tried to keep my mind clear and attentive and worry-free. And even now when I reflect on the experience, I feel time waves are being shown to me again and again and the vision pops up very vividly. And with it the hoping and praying for a better time for all human kind. Tick-tock, tick-tock, I made the encounter at 11-10-12.

What clockwork this universe is; the calculations in my doctorate turned out to be a question of 1-0 or 1-2. No forgetting that. The world went digital. Computers, cellphones and the rest of digital electronics being based on a binary numeral system with 2 at its core and gate values using 1 and 0. What a progressive matrix behind our modern way of life, the design of which was sought back to Indian mathematician of antiquity, Pingala.

Kalachakra, the great vehicle of Time and Time cycles, is both the paradox of modern time and great revelation.

# Let It Be

I walk the temple grounds in wonder while adjusting to the Brahmin's garland. I feel bathed in flowers as water from them drips on me. No operating manual for entering and no money involved either at that magical Vishwanath lingam when I was given the garland. I had felt pretty free of possessions upon this first encounter and was not asking for anything, I had come in praise, but was given abundantly instead. Am I okey with things the way they are? Just let it be. Try to stay focused and free of the usual mind chatter. Silently commute with the skies above, or is this a subconscious prayer to the heavens? A mysterious jyotir pond somewhere out there?

*Let it be, let it be,*
*whispering words of wisdom,*
*let it be.*

*And in my hour of darkness*
*Mother Mary comes to me...*

According to the ancient sages, having tasted the nectar, there is no turning back: *Om Shanti*. I now walk to the jyotir shrine akin to the Golden Temple where there is a young Brahmin who encourages me to keep repeating the Om Shanti mantra. Outside, I halt and take a look at how the whole platform is designed. It's beautiful and laid with marble tiles, everything in here is grey-in-white beneath an open sky with mud and leaves scattered around--some natural decor. I am glad for the simplicity of it. The black flag of Shiva on the guilded spire of the Golden Temple serves for grandeur. But the Vishwanath lingam is of such universal force that I keep stumbling.

After some contemplation on a stone bench, I head for the third shrine. Noone is here. I am alone with a lingam for the first time, offering some green leaves. A trancelike sense and timelessness engulfs me but a swirm of mosquitos disturbs my peace and I head out. The blue and white sky above the courtyard is covered in some glimmering streaks. Sunset falls. A monkey appears out of nowhere and grabs a bag of nuts from my basket, then disappears in a glance. He looks sharp in his swift manners and quite dignified. Clearly at home here in this holiest temple of all. What marvel. This offering of nuts comes very naturally and now I feel my visit is completed and I feel ready to turn back.

Young monks in orange call to me politely and ask if *everything is okey mam*? I take one last look around whilst staying under a sheltered roof to the right with other devotees, all from India, then leave enclothed in one heartwarming garland of leaves and flowers, the size of myself. I've been given new clothing--some alive clothing--in this ancient forest city of Bliss. I thank the Lord but wonder if it is I or the garland who shall do the walk home to Monu. *You can talk the talk, but can you walk the walk*, the saying goes in Stanley Kubrick's *Full Metal Jacket*. I come to think of it: Nature is the companion who never leaves us.

# The Heart of the Matter

I managed back to Monu walking in garland or in the *walk-in garland*. The Lord longs for a pure devoted and kind heart, no fuzzy ceremonies for Vishwanath, or pomps. That's all there is to it, or that was at least my experience. The garland I was given has the same colors as the deities wear and one sees in pictures of them at Monu such as garlands on Krishna and Radha, same make and color arrangements, innermost white, then marooni and yellow, with green leaves outmost, all silver-threaded. This is clearly an ancient custom alive and thriving.

My heart ponders and pulsates blood throughout, it somehow feels like I've dived into the veins of Anapurna, the great giver of life. Dog barking, music playing, and I keep sipping lots of drinking water out of a plastic bottle; one's physical being is almost a total water make-up anyhow. Fresh flow of blood keeps streaming in the heart, brain and body. And, the dog next door howls to some Beatles music now playing at Yogi Lodge, what a character this funny dog:

*I wanna hold your hand*
*and when I touch you*
*I'll be laughing*

*and when I touch you*
*I feel happy inside.*

Sure, Sumana has been touched. Some self-transform in a true present via a flower garland blessed by a stone from heaven, one jyotir Vishwanath. Here in this ancient city, there is much grace in everything with death around the corner. The garland shall wither and die and so shall I. Pure grace.

# Anapurna and Recycling

Cows sniff at piles of flowers left along gali sides. Flowers used for decorative and devotional purposes, some once were Hibiscus flowers of Shiva garlands. Occasionally, cows and bulls are seen eating out of the piles, mostly the green leaves of Anandhakhan. Later we'll have milk and curd from these dissolving joys and tears of bhakti. Goddess Anapurna - the holy cow - is given the duty of feeding all beings and is extremely economical and smart at it. Life moves in mysterious ways and here is recycling at its best.

I had this dream of grandma Ingibjorg. A sweet aura of quietude swept through me. I had been at her deathbed; she had been the first person whose dying and blissful crossing I had experienced. Her mild presence is here now with the feel of loving kindness. Her passion for botany and her way of seeing Nature as sacred always moved me. And her husband sea captain grandpa, sailed the seas trusting his dreams for direction. People like grandma Ingibjorg are true bhaktis in their lives without ever knowing or boasting of it. A great reader and a mystic too. She had taught me all I know about Egypt, the pyramids, secret teachings, the starry skies, the Mayas and the Hopis.

In the dream she was showing me periods in my life in a fleeting mirror--the paths I've walked with their twists and turns. And in the blink of an eye, I am here and now in Kashi. The paths I've taken leave me completed and happy in this ancient City of Light. I guess I am recycling.

*Knock, knock, knock*
*on Heaven's door...*

Last night my sleep was on and off with bathroom visits. A noise got me fully awake at dawn, a birdvoice cut the sky going on for a while, then others joined in a cheerful chorus. At half past six the temple bells started chiming the day in and soon one could hear people on the streets, some busily sweeping the galis. After his howling concerto last night, the dog now keeps quiet. Ah, how good it is to have that brisk morning shower. Let Ganga purify body and soul and make my day. She always does.

Today is Friday and upcoming Sunday with its new moon is Durga's festival day October 14--Durga who willingly threw Herself into the universe to fight evil--and I'll be leaving so it's time to go shopping. No grand gifts as I have some luggage already and leave some with Ramesh until next time. I hope my stomach gets better today though, not all that bad.

Kashi keeps playing on my guts in many ways after witnessing galaxy swirls and aeons of time or yugas at the Vishwanath jyotir in the Golden Temple. No wonder one feels dizzy when creation and time ticks into one's staring face; strange how the deep prayers are surfaced here at the Ganga and the Golden Temple. I had prayed for answers about time and evolution: where is this world going? Out of known space and into unknown space, it seems, and times are changing. The world rocks. Shifts and reforms on such deep levels call for us to centre ourselves and find faith and love and compassion amongst turmoil no matter what.

# Ganga Devi

Cowsmouth or *Gaumukh* in sanskrit is the name of the cave in the Gangroti Himalayan glacier wherefrom the Ganga emerges, running in one mesmerizing flow towards the *Ganga Sagar* in the Bay of Bengal. The trees at her farther bank look like a flowing stairway to heaven in the morning mist. Ganga is a goddess sister of Parvati and a symbol of purity. No wonder Her waters are believed to bring liberation or moksha to people. That She is thought to form a sacred bridge between this world and the next and that bathing here is believed to bring liberation from the cycle of births and ease the journey to the great Hereafter. I am getting familiar with Her banks covered with rows of stonesteps which sweep down ghat after ghat where one can watch a great panorma of the joys of life and the sorrows of death. What highroad of Nature who has triggered the growth of civilization. What web Kashi.

A waking dream surfaces, one I had during a visit to the old Rolduc monastery in Holland in June 2011. At which time I had given a talk on dreams in the Icelandic Sagas. After climbing a long and lofty staircase towards the sky, I had entered my grandma's cottage. Later in the dream, I had seen a ripe meadow and softly blowing grain in a gentle wind (like a tranquil riverflow) when I meditated on a multidimensional picture of a female saint inside the cottage. I had wondered then what it meant and I feel I now hold the answer.

In my dream vision last night, I saw a creature in the Ganga looking like a dolphin upon which, I awoke startled, saying to myself, no that can't be, a dolphin here in such a southern warm place! But today I learn of the *Makara*, a mythical river creature in the sacred Ganga river that seems to be a mix of a crocodile and a dolphin!

There is a small neat shrine on Monu's wall by the entrance to the right with beautiful ceramic tiles covering the shrine on the inside. A very old shrine they say with goddess Ganga presented with two mythical figures for protection at each of her side, one is the Makara. This is the first and only shrine I have encountered so far here in Kashi figuring Ganga in her goddess form, and it is near the end of my stay. How wonderful and simply elegant but how blind we are most of the time to life's little surprises in front of us.

# Divine Ferryman and Eternal Yogi

Flowing waters can cast a spell and Ganga has mesmerized me for life. Living here feels like being in another age and time. A song from Brihadaranyaka Uphanishad comes to mind:

*O Lord; From untruth*
*Lead me to truth.*
*From darkness (ignorance)*
*Lead me to light (knowledge).*
*From death lead me*
*to immortality.*

As Tarakeshwara, Lord Shiva is the divine ferryman who rows the souls of the dead across the river to heaven, all the while singing the Taraka mantra of liberation. At Yogi Lodge tonight over dinner, I caught a glimpse of a passed woman, bathed in light and wondered if her cremation had just taken place? And if she was somehow connected to people at the Lodge?

I am realizing better how often this City of Light has been under attack in the course of history and hence how often it has had to rebuild herself. What survivor. It has no surviving temples prior to the 18th century. How eternal this city of weaving amidst forces of creation and destruction--weaving the threads of life and death alike. Kashi weavers began by weaving the silks for deities and priests and they were famous for the fineness of their cotton textiles from early on. The cloth covering Buddha's body upon death was woven by them and was said to be so fine that it did not even absorb oil. In the time of Buddha, Kashi was a wealthy city of commerce, it was safe and pleasant and Ganga was a famous route of trade.

Kashi is Shiva's city and still an important centre of traditional learning like yoga. Shiva is the lord of the Yogis as He meditates in the mountainheights of Kailash and occasionally pays His material abode at Ganga a visit. So Shiva's city is naturally a centre of the science and philosophy of yoga. Shiva is said to have founded the system of yoga and his consort Parvati is said to have been his first disciple.

As enunciated in the Uphanishads, achieving a pure consciousness, is central to the philosophy of Yoga. Many of the Uphanishads were composed in Kashi, hence a centre of yoga from the beginning. Here, people celebrate not only life but the journey ahead of the soul after the transfer between worlds. The spirituality of the Westernes who visit is much more discreet and I don't know if they take to the old cosmology but it is the progressive move forward that really matters, is it not? They seem quite dedicated.

Regarding spirituality, people the world over seem to be going in a more othodox way than before. It makes me wonder and worry if this trend paves way for more fundamentalist values and eventually causes a rift in our societies and threatens humane values?

# Vehicles of Evolution

Now the bells are chiming at Kali Temple or perhaps it is the Golden Temple? It is half past nine. Half-damaged people in a broken world need decent sleep. The dreaming dog is whining and grunting, perhaps having nightmares. Kashi has left a deep and lasting impression, and this surround and community has been exceptionally benevolent and provided all the help I've needed. Hence I feel safe and blessed. After good sleep this night, the swallows are tweeding happily to a beautiful, sunny day.

Much cultural diversity in terms of dreams and dreaming and multiple sources of research into dreams exist globally. Among these tools are surveys and questionnairies, long-term journals, sleeplab experiments, psychotherapeutic case studies, historical texts and cross-cultural reports. Within this context, one finds accounts of extraordinary but rare dreams that have been life-changing such as for dreamers in India and Iceland alike. Jung spoke of these life-changing dreams as *Big dreams* and defined them as rare but unusually vivid and highly arousing dreams. A lasting impact is made on the dreamer's waking consciousness.

Theology professor and former president of IASD, Kelly Bulkeley at the Graduate Theological Union (GTU) in Berkeley, speaks of several forms of big dreams and states that these dreams tend to physically arouse surges of emotion both positive and negative, amazing visual imagery, feelings of intense realism, and, or, striking interactions with powerful beings. Further, they have the tangible effect of expanding the individual's range of imaginative understanding and in some cases his or her spiritual sensitivity.

(It had been at Berkeley where my parents-in-law first met--both had come to study--Winston studied philosophy here and Johann studied English-American literature. And it was to Berkeley that I came for my first conference on dreams in 2003, as hosted by the IASD. Johann became the editor-in-chief for the English-Icelandic dictionary, a post he took over from S. Sörenson whose wife, Ingibjorg, translated the Autobiography of a Yogi, into Icelandic).

The strong carry-over efffects associated with big dreams may offer clues to the evolutionary processes by which dreaming contributes to human survival and healthy functioning according to Bulkeley. He speaks of mystical dreams as being at the upper end of the elemental states that involve the carry-over effects of big dreams and that mystic dreams express the human capacity to envision a transcendental freedom from the oppressive limitations of gravity, entropy and death.

Some such examples are flying dreams that give the dreamer a vivid physiological experience of being liberated from the bonds of earthly existence, says Bulkeley, other examples, are visitation dreams in which the dreamer encounters deceased loved ones whose living presence defies the finality of physical death; healing dreams which bring tangible relief from mental and or physical suffering are still other examples. Among those transformative dreams are ecstatic dreams of brilliant light, lucid self-awareness and divine union, along with aesthetically creative dreams of astonishing beauty and cosmic harmony.

In concluding, Bulkeley further argues that the central function of big dreams and mystical dreams may be the one of making the brain grow with lasting effects on human neurology and adjustment. Such dreams may turn out to be vehicles for growth and evolution in all fields of human existence. The message is clear from the gift of dreaming: we must cherish our dreams in order to grow in this broken world and evolve with life on the planet and in the universe.

# Cottage Emporium and Mahesh

A soft Friday morning has broken, and I head for the Silk Emporium Cottage. I've been in before to have a look. This time to buy some simple and pretty little gifts. I have not wanted money and material things to engulf my life while over.

While wrapping up the gifts, I chat with the young shopkeeper in the front room downstairs, he says he has spent time in Europe. On the wall, I notice a picture of Maharishi Mahesh yogi, the guru of the Beatles taken at a Kumbh Mela, probably in 2001 when it was last held. The greatest one for one hundred and fourty years--a Maha Kumbh Mela is taking place in a few months in Allahabad. The posters for it are on display at Monu.

Maharishi died some three years ago, the young shopkeeper informs me, but he still has a large ashram in Holland. This goodlooking and polite young man who helps me finalise the shopping now tells me all about his family. That his father has for long been a great devotee of Maharishi and gave up everything to follow him and went to live at the ashram in Holland many years ago and that later his wife - mother of the young shopkeeper - accompanied him. This is the reason why their two sons where left to run the shop. *Mixed feelings, but such is the life of many devotees*, he explains, *full of paradoxes*. He did not like it too much in the European ashram either, *it was ok but all felt somewhat flat, both the landscape and daily life*, and he missed the hustle and bustle of Varanasi. With a grin on his face, he admits he should do more meditation though.

Incidentally, I had been close by Maharishi's ashram last Summer when staying at the old medieval monastery Rolduc in Kerkrade. I had been there to give a talk at an international dream conference. The focus was on dreams in our Sagas and on our ancestress Gudrun of the Laxdaela clan during medival times in West Iceland and her gift of dreaming.

Yeah; it is both interesting and surprising to find the story of Maharishi Mahesh who takes his name after Mahesh, the fourth god in the Hindu godhead, in a silk shop. The young shopkeeper now starts telling me about Varanasi and speaks of the need to clean the city and tells me of their friend for many years, a Spanish writer who has lived here for over twenty years. Varanasi certainly needs cleaning in many ways, no doubting that. What honorable project of cleaning the shrines and temples of Kashi and bring in fresh special paint for Lady Bright.

# Bathing in Light and Water

I enjoyed breakfast at Yogi's while *Shine on me* was playin'. Outside I see the white cow and calf. A soft warm light shines down on mother and son this morning. Every move is beamed upon when they head for their usual place in the gali. Once at the river, there is a spectacular play of colors. Ganga reminds of the Milky Way on Earth--what energy, what force--with ligths beaming out of Her waters in different shades of milky pastel. I bathe in light and water crystals. And the sand and clay at Her banks feel newly refreshed and warm. The whole universe hails.

Boys play with kites at the Shiva Temple up front, partially submerged in the holy river. Agni, the God of Fire, was born here. Animal Tamer would love to come and play with kites as he does at home in Iceland and also learn to speak with the animals who always are around down by Ganga.

A young girl sells me postcards of lanterns at sunset over Ganga, lanterns being put out by widows to memorise their deceased husbands. Let the lantern aloft and afloat on the River of Gods and she shall make the transfer to her loved ones. It feels like true and unconditional love for the Supreme exists in humans after all.

I come to think of all the history that has taken place down by the sacred river. However, Indian history is a scattered venue as few have bothered to chronicle the past. Religion is ever vibrant, a multi-hued synthesis in this City of Light; I guess travelling here for some participant observation to see how people view their world is a good way to read Kashi's history, past and present. I have conversed with Kashi in wake and dreams between India and Iceland; in this travelogue of mine, one must visualise the eternal city and the panorama of Ganges. A way of dreaming.

# Flyin' with the Lord most High

Strolling down the galis has a dreamlike quality (albeit too crowded for an ordinary dreamscape). Sometimes I feel like flyin' with my steps very light on the downtrodden mudpaths of age-old galis. On my way home to Monu, I *fly* by Babu's to bid last farewell and watch more photos of him and Goldie. I'll buy a sari from him when I shall be back next time, a proper clothing for a lady shahib.

Mahesh is the one God of the Hindu pantheon that I was not particularly familiar with before coming, meaning *Lord most high*. Already at the start of my flight London - Delhi, Mahesh reminded of Himself through the Lady Punjab sitting next to me in seat 44A, an empty seat was left between us on a full plane at 44B. Empty spaces in wake and dreams are symbolic of new beginnings; do we bother to notice that Mahesh may actually fly with us? The most supreme and highest reality according to Hindu belief, or so I gather. A simple meditation and bakhti on a jet plane where I learn in the silent mudra way from a Punjab lady that the guru of the Beatles is only one expression of named Mahesh.

Mahesh is mentioned in the Mahabharata with its Bhagavad Gita written around 400 AD. The epic and gita have played a strong role in my life since adolescence with their *strange heroic whispers from the twilight of the world.* I realize Mahesh has been with me all along, I just failed to notice. Mahesh has now helped me reconnect with *aham*--our deep spiritual union with ourselves and the universe.

# Boots are Made for Walking

I am on my final stroll and this time in the other direction to the market along Vishwanath gali. Then I take an opposite turn to the circuit at Baba Black Sheep. *These boots are made for walking*: wealth should be distributed in a world needing unity and some of it is seen here on the markets and gali stalls. I end with buying not boots but traditional open shoes for a little lady at home, they are brocaded as well (very Kashi like).

Out of the narrow dim galis and into the main street a blue sky breaks with the sun soon setting. The mainstreet buildings feel closer in the twilight, many are quite pretty and some must have been grandiose houses of the nobility or even been small palaces in Kashi's bygone days of glory. If washed and painted they would look great but at same time risk loosing that charm of being ancient and forlorn, my first impression upon arrival. Every day I learn more about the galis and the people at the market stalls and now I learn the names of the four main ghats all signposted where I stand.

It's late afternoon or around half past five and people are already flocking down to the river for aarti and the fire ceremony at seven. Well, I still should have time before all the spaces are filled in to sit down there and cast a last glance at Ganga's mesmerising flow, bid farewell. Some boats are already out with devotees. The river flow feels mysteriously dark-blue and I spot floating candleligths, offerings to the sacred river. In an hour everything will be crowded and Agni will be praised.

# Master at Shrine and River

Then he passed me. It was the last day of my stay in the City of Light. But as I walked again leaving the stall where I had been shopping for gifts, he stopped at a small stall in front of me, sat down there, said something to the shopkeeper, his face half-hid but looked attentive behind white. All cloaked in clean white. And now as I pass I catch a glimpse of his face, beautiful eyes and a beard. Great serenity; elegantly tall--a slender figure.

Who can he be? Earlier when I had first seen him, he had been standing at a shrine lost in prayer, pure devotion pouring from his eyes. No theatricals. Later that day I found out, it had been a shrine to Ganesha. Seeing this stream of true and honest devotion springing forth while doing his bhakti reminded me of the white cow in the Kalika gali with her baby calf and the abundant love she bestows on him. Baby Nandi. Her eyes float in love.

They say true masters take many forms when visiting Kashi. I start believing in humankind again. He reminds me of the man in white standing at the riverbank towards Assighat--or was it a fleeting dream--the eve I had been up and down Ganga in the motor boat to Varuna Bridge then making a sharp turn over to Assighat. Afterwards sailing back to where we had started to attend the ceremony at Dashaswameth with Ramesh and the angelic boatman and his teenage son, boatman to be.

That was the eve of having those two young tourist girls in full gear and latest gadget hopping unto the boat for photographing the whole ceremony without bothering to leave space for the humble devotees in our boat and other boats to watch in peace and awe. Some of whom have come here for this ceremony of a lifetime after much hard work. I asked them to sit down, a mudra did the trick. Is living in a virtual reality – a panoramic photographic world - more important than the real thing?

# A Blessing from Anapurna

Leaving Yogi Lodge after breakfast the last morning to lock my suitcases for the airport, I notice that the door to the white Shiva Temple opposite Monu is open and that somebody is inside. I guess it is the Brahmin priest whom I had met inside the temple the other day and have since seen around a few times, once buying dairy milk chockolates from the tiny stall close to the shrine to Ganga Devi. At the breakfast an elderly man dressed in an olive kakhi suit suddenly appears quite noble looking. He passes me at my restaurant table and looks me in the eye. I wonder if here we finally have the private owner of that white Shiva Temple opposite Monu? Perhaps the owner of the cattle too?

From the very onset of my stay, I have noticed the white cow and baby calf and talked to her softly and petted on her forehead. Now upon leaving and having a final chat in Ramesh's shop with him and Amitir from Yogi Lodge, a boy appears out of the blue in the doorway. I ask his name, he says a name I do not hear properly and then *Garon*. Amitir laughs and says he is the boy who milks the white cow and plays with kites. And that he now calls himself Garon because his dog died yesterday who had been called Garon.

The young cowherd smiles and leaves happy after I talk to him about his deceased dog and the cow he cares so well for.

I feel the white cow is sending me a final farewell; a blessing from Anapurna who beholds all the gods within, a true bearer of unbound compassion.

# A Dharma-Dog and his Brahmin Owner

A beautiful half-clouded morning has broken and it is not too hot. Will I see the Ganga from the plane this Sunday when flying back to Delhi? Time, or perhaps Ganga Devi-- the River of Time--has turned the tide again, and I rejoice, feeling better prepared to face what comes. This has been the pilgrimage of a lifetime that so many Hindus prepare and yearn for all their lives eventually to visit Kashi and bathe in the holy waters of Ganga Mai. But hey, I am an accidental Hindu too with all the rest I may be, or become.

And, finally, I have learned that *Chack* aka *Jazz* is the name of the dog next door, and Chack now barks his farewell. He gives a last blessing to the shahib at Monu tuning in with *Those were the best days of my life*, now playing at Yogi Lodge. You surely have helped materialize the truth of the Bhagavad Gita, namely, that *dharma* follows one through a lifetime like a faithful dog. When fairness of conduct is lost, lack of compassion and mercy results.

I am very grateful for your company in this ancient abode of the Lord, Chack-Jazz. And soon your brahmin owner, Prashant Mishra, is taking me to the airport with

Ramesh. (Reflecting on precognition in dreams, I now feel Ramish is the named Kristinn--someone devoted to the Lord--in my first dream at Monu, and Prashant the young man with papers in the hospital-university dream of my workplace). Together they head the much needed Black Kashi Project of keeping Ganga pure.

My visit has ended and on my way to the airport, the young brahmin gives me the Kashi mantra ever to cherish in my heart...

# Namaskar

It's getting cooler. My Transfer scarf of Shiva design comes in handy. We sail above cloud levels with Surya, the sun, shining bright. Beneath us, grand cloud formations look like an ethereal city above the city with Ganga glittering through and through. Namaskar City of Light and River of Time.

A fiery pillar flashes across the sky towards the Himalayas and the Master takes to His Heavenly abode.

# Acknowledgements

Heartfelt thanks to my family and friends
for believing in my dreams.
And to my Kashi friends, Ramesh, Prashant,
Amitir, Madhav, Indu and Monu,
Kailash and Babú, for their benevolence and great help.